Softworld 2.1 : The Imperial Message
WEXNER CENTER FOR THE ARTS / THE OHIO STATE UNIVERSITY

Produced in association with
Softworld 2.1: The Imperial Message
May 14–July 31, 1994
Wexner Center for the Arts
The Ohio State University

Organized by Sarah J. Rogers, Wexner Center Director
of Exhibitions.

The exhibition and related residency and education
programs were made possible by the Wexner Center
Foundation and Battelle Endowment for Technology
and Human Affairs. Additional support for the
development of *The Imperial Message* came from Kubota
Pacific Corporation, Blue Sky Productions, Sony
Corporation, Sense 8 Corporation, Elias Associates,
Imtech Corporation, Virtual Research, IBM, Polhemus
Inc., MicroSoft Corporation, Crystal River Engineering,
and Phar Lap Software. Additional support for
education programs came from the Ohio Joint Program
in the Arts and Humanities.

Graphic Designer: M. Christopher Jones
Editor: Ann Bremner

Additional Illustration Credits

The illustrations captioned *The Imperial Message: Set
Concept #1* (pp. 29, 31–32) are by Brian D'Amato.
Dimensions are as follows: 16 ¼ x 20 ½" (p. 29);
16 ¼ x 19 ½" (p. 31, bottom left); 13 ¼ x 20" (p. 31,
bottom right); 10 ⅛ x 18 ½" (p. 32).

The computer-generated images from *The Imperial
Message* (pp. 29–35, cover) were rendered at Blue Sky
Productions' CGI Studio™ under the direction of
Michael Ferraro and Janine Cirincione.

"Virtual Kafka" from *Stan Mack's Real Life Funnies*
(p. 64) originally appeared in the *Village Voice*, April 26,
1994. It is reproduced by permission of Stan Mack.

The photograph of Softworlds, Inc. (back cover) is by
Timothy Greenfield-Sanders. Pictured, left to right, are
Michael Ferraro, Brian D'Amato, and Janine Cirincione.

Published by
Wexner Center for the Arts
The Ohio State University
North High Street at Fifteenth Avenue
Columbus, Ohio 43210-1393

ISBN: 1-881390-07-1

Cover image: *The Imperial Message*
The Empire (birdseye view)
model shot, 1994

Foreword

As a contemporary arts center with programs that span the visual, performative, and media arts, the Wexner Center for the Arts is particularly interested in seeking out and supporting projects that exist at crossroads, junctures, and interstices between disciplines. A special impetus toward multi-disciplinary or multimedia presentations has long fueled the trajectory of contemporary art and has appropriately energized the Wexner Center's programming since its inception. To date, however, works that might more properly be described as interdisciplinary or intermedia (taking place, that is, in the not-easily-definable space between disciplines, media, genre) have been a less frequent, if no less intriguing, part of the mix. Thus it is a special pleasure for us to introduce the work of Softworlds, Inc., recipient of the Wexner Center's 1993–94 Residency Award in the visual arts. Softworlds is a collaborative research studio for the development and publication of interactive, computer-based art. While mapping the expansive new territories of interactive computer technologies such as virtual reality, the artists of Softworlds by necessity occupy many points of intersection: between art and science, between narrative and symbolic communication, among visual, performative, literary, design, and media arts. In fact, Janine Cirincione, Brian D'Amato, and Michael Ferraro, the members of Softworlds, describe their Wexner Center residency endeavor, *Softworld 2.1: The Imperial Message*, as lying "somewhere between architecture, film, and game."

The Imperial Message is an interactive virtual-reality experience inspired by Franz Kafka's parable "An Imperial Message." Kafka's story, in which a messenger sets off to bring a crucial message from a dying emperor to a distant subject, is an eloquent meditation on the fragility of communication and the tenuous nature of the ties between governments and their citizens. Softworlds' *The Imperial Message* further explores those ideas while expanding upon their implications for the very technology the group utilizes. Cirincione, D'Amato, and Ferraro endeavor to bring aesthetic, critical, and theoretical perspectives to bear on this work, moving beyond the appeal of new technology (such as virtual reality) used for its own sake. They are attracted by the potential for interactivity inherent in the model of computer games, but they are also interested in exploring different kinds of narrative techniques and creating evocative visual "realities" as settings for interactive "computer-fictions" such as *The Imperial Message.* This new project is the centerpiece of Softworlds' Wexner Center exhibition, which also features *Softworld 1.2: Sacrifice,* an earlier computer "game" developed by the group.

So many individuals and groups have contributed in one way or another to the realization of Softworlds' residency project and exhibition that it would be impossible to name them all, although the artists have clearly endeavored to be comprehensive in their acknowledgments at the back of this volume. Nonetheless, special—and in some cases repeated—thanks are resoundingly due to a few crucial supporters and members of the team. As a Wexner Center Residency Award project, the development of *The Imperial Message* has been made possible in large part by the Wexner Center Foundation, and we wish to first express our ongoing gratitude to the members of the foundation's board of trustees, especially Chairman Leslie H. Wexner and President Ric Wanetik. The residency award program, which enables the Wexner Center to provide substantive technical, financial, and creative support directly to artists, is a superb example of cultural patronage and one that greatly enriches this institution, its audience, and the larger realm of creative endeavor. Generous support from the Battelle Endowment for Technology and Human Affairs also has been critical in bringing this project to fruition. Education programs associated with the exhibition have been funded, in part, by the Ohio Joint Program in the Arts and Humanities. In addition, several corporations have provided equipment and services directly to Softworlds, and the Wexner Center joins the artists in expressing thanks to Kubota Pacific Corporation, Blue Sky Productions, Sony Corporation, Sense 8 Corporation, Elias Associates, Imtech Corporation, Virtual Research, IBM, Polhemus Inc., MicroSoft Corporation, Crystal River Engineering, and Phar Lap Software.

For their exceptionally spirited and provocative contributions to this publication, we thank Michael Benedikt and Peter Halley, whose essays vividly illuminate the ideas behind Softworlds' work. Perhaps more importantly, each author deftly places those ideas within larger constellations of contemporary thought regarding the collisions and collusions of culture and technology. We are also most grateful to our colleagues at The Ohio State University and the members of the Columbus community who have assisted with and participated in Softworlds residency activities. Director Wayne E. Carlson and Matthew R. Lewis, of Ohio State's Advanced Computing Center for the Arts and Design, and Professors Richard Roth and Susan King Roth, of the university's Center for Interdisciplinary Studies in Art and Design, have been particularly supportive and helpful.

At the Wexner Center itself, the elaborate networking intrinsic to Softworlds' working method has resulted in an especially large and diverse project staff, admirably orchestrated and energetically coordinated by Sarah J. Rogers, Director of Exhibitions. Sarah has spearheaded this residency from its inception over eighteen months ago. A full roster of those most closely involved in the project is included elsewhere in the catalogue, but special acknowledgments should go to Education and Technology Liaison Carol Gigliotti, to Steve Jones, Kathleen Kopp, and Michael A. Lucas—the trio who ably led the technical and installation team for the exhibition—and to Ann Bremner, Robert Brooks, Melodie Calvert, Timothy Frank, Bill Horrigan, M. Christopher Jones, Annetta Massie, Patricia Trumps, and Sean Ulmer. We are also most appreciative of the efforts of Carol Gigliotti's creative students Eric Zimmerman, Todd Sines, and Tony Ramos, who assisted in the development and distribution of publicity materials for the exhibition.

Finally, of course, I offer my utmost thanks, and those of the entire Wexner Center staff, to Janine Cirincione, Brian D'Amato, and Michael Ferraro of Softworlds, for a residency experience that has epitomized the challenges and rewards of exploring and even temporarily "occupying" that mysterious space at the crossroads.

Sherri Geldin, *Director*

Conflicts and Confluences

Art and technology. Both possess the potential to change our view of the world, and to do so, sometimes, in an instant. Functioning as a model for imagery and experience, the aesthetic or technological event (especially as digital art) stimulates the senses, the emotions, and the intellect. Both can nourish and guide us; both are empowering forces. With such shared qualities, we could assume that art and tech are close and fruitful collaborators. Too often, however, we perceive these arenas as separate, foreign, and impenetrable. Perhaps this breakdown in communication begins with the jargon associated with each camp, terms which can be quite intimidating: *CGI real-time systems, HMDs, total-immersive feedback systems,* and *cyberspace* describe aspects of recent advancements in digital technology; *appropriation, post-structuralist art, deconstructivist analysis,* and *multidisciplinary environmental installation* define currents in recent artistic activity. Such words, whether theoretical or merely descriptive, however, describe concepts that are connected. *Total-immersive systems* and *environmental installations* both circumscribe experiences that are multisensory and physically inclusive for the viewer. And *CGI* and *appropriation* are each creative means to expand the possibilities of image making. But for individuals involved in either the arts or computers, the jargon associated with the other discipline can spark fear and a reluctance to search for meanings beyond the language codes. Thanks to such schisms, territories have been delineated: those in the arts often denigrate endeavors by technology-based individuals as not intellectually or aesthetically valuable. Those in technology see artists and the art community as inept and incapable of understanding the true potential offered by their media. The end result is a bit of phobia on each side, as both feel they may loose something by corroborating with the "enemy." In some respects, this tension is healthy: a dynamic necessary to any exploration that promises to mine new resources. In other regards, this separation of arts and sciences is a modern, and ultimately misguided, phenomenon.

Further complicating this scenario is the widespread hype surrounding another set of terms whose definitions are elusive: *interactivity, virtual reality, information superhighway, CD-ROM.* The dramatic emphasis on technology's place in our lives, whether touted by the Vice President of the United States or exploited by telephone and entertainment companies, has (as happens with all emerging technologies) added to the confusion. The hype terrifies those who envision computers taking away our humanity and discourages the artistic and intellectual communities from embracing this realm as theirs. It also encumbers those in the trenches of technology, who are often pushed to pursue newness at the expense of thorough investigation. Children are the segment of the population least self-conscious and perhaps most comfortable in straddling these worlds. For most kids, computers, Game-boys, Disneyland, or a good book all exist on the same level—as entertainments or tools, as elements of their world. One does not necessarily supersede the other: kids don't celebrate technology for its own sake, nor do they refuse to allow it in their lives.

However, there are groups of adults braving these rough waters and leading what is a paradigmatic shift in the realm of art and technology. These current efforts are certainly not without precedents. Interactivity, virtual worlds, and art-science hybrids all have roots in a range of sources. Italian masques and Renaissance spectacles, for example, were essentially interactive events combining theater with many arts and entertainment forms. The Russian Constructivists employed the vocabulary of design, architecture, painting, and sculpture to redirect the physical and social fabric of life, thus inventing means through which the arts interacted in daily events. Happenings in the 1950s, earthworks of the 1960s and 1970s, video, and performance art all sought to extract the essence of interactivity (even though the experiences were not defined by this term). Concepts of virtual worlds have had a range of sources in the imagination, via—for instance—the French Surrealists' collaborations that engaged dreams, intuition, and psychological realms as artistic media. In more concrete terms, dioramas and World Fairs constructed other worlds, other kinds of reality, through which visitors could journey. Additionally, advancements in film and photography made the realities of daily

life "virtual" in these art forms: the serial photographs of
Eadweard Muybridge articulated the details of physical
movement; the filmic experiments of the Lumière brothers
documented the daily activities of workers or the speed of
steam engines. Other pioneering ventures specifically linked
the arts and sciences: the activities of EAT (Experiments in
Art and Technology) or Gyorgy Kepes and Otto Piene's
efforts at the Center for Advanced Visual Studies at the
Massachusetts Institute of Technology, which encouraged
fellows to develop work in association with the artistic and
scientific communities. In 1970 the *Art and Technology*
exhibition for the world's fair in Osaka, Japan, and the Los
Angeles County Museum of Art paired artists (such as Andy
Warhol) and industries in the creative process. Today, many
observers commonly perceive any version of interactivity as
an exchange *between* two or more conditions: a vague
transaction that happens in the gulf between the participants. What is becoming clear is that the dramatic import of
this realm is found in interactivity's literal definition: a series
of occurrences that act *on* each party with the potential to
persuade, to convert, or to conquer.

Particularly baffling for both those within and outside the
world of technology is the concept of *virtual reality.* Science
fiction writer William Gibson defined the concept of virtual
reality, or VR, in his 1984 novel *Neuromancer* as an artificial
world through which humans navigate, responding to an
architectural structure or parallel universe that is digital,
not physical. Precedents for VR-type experiences abound—
Dorothy's Oz or Alice's Wonderland in literature,
Tomorrowland at Disneyland, flight simulators for the
military. But today, the misguided expectation that VR will
replace actual reality causes terror and jubilation concur-
rently, and appropriately raises questions about how technology will, and should, affect communications, education, war,
social orders, design, architecture, art, and even sex. As
Brenda Laurel, the most vigilant field reporter on VR, has
continually observed, these issues all ultimately question
control—how, why, and by whom these devices and their
content are co-opted and nurtured.[1]

Against this backdrop has evolved the work of three individuals collectively known as Softworlds, Inc. The three who

1. The "Suggestions for Further
Reading" at the back of this
catalogue include writings by both
William Gibson and Brenda Laurel
and offer a brief, introductory
overview of this vast subject.

currently compose the group, Janine Cirincione, Brian D'Amato, and Michael Ferraro, together personify the conflicts and confluences of creating new works in the digital realm. Softworlds was formed in 1992 to publish and create interactive art projects. At that time, it was Cirincione, D'Amato, and Dr. Michael Spertus, a mathematician from Princeton University and author of the computer language BRAID, who participated in an exhibition curated by Cirincione at Jack Tilton Gallery in New York City. The exhibition *Through the Looking Glass: Artists' First Encounters with Virtual Reality* presented a lively selection of artists exploring the aesthetic potential of VR: from pioneers in this realm Myron Krueger, Jaron Lanier, and William Gibson/ Dennis Asbaugh to newcomers Matt Mullican, Nicole Stenger, and D'Amato. The first such exhibition in a New York art gallery, *Through the Looking Glass* attempted to bridge the schism between art and tech and to educate each camp about the remarkable potential of the other, especially when pursued in collaboration. D'Amato's contribution to the show was a selection of story board drawings shown in book form and a video fly-through of what he called *The Sacrifice Game.* Around this time, Cirincione met Ferraro, an artist who had created interactive installations with computers through the 1970s and was then Systems Architect at Blue Sky Productions, one of the most advanced computer animation studios in the country. Shortly there-after, these three came together to develop *The Sacrifice Game,* which they described as a "fully interactive text and image exploration game." *Softworld 1.2: Sacrifice* premièred at The New Museum in May 1993 as part of the *Final Frontier* exhibition, which loosely charted the art world's perceptions of art engaged at the frontier of technology.

In great part, the group's success is due to these three individuals' varying backgrounds and interests, their mutual understanding and expertise in the artistic and intellectual, as well as technical, aspects of their endeavors, and the seamlessness of *their* interactions. The individual contributions to each phase of a project are not assigned, separate tasks. Rather, decisions—from shaping the narrative, to sketching a feature of the landscape, to determining which hardware system will best present the software—are reached through a fluid exchange and discussion. In effect, like three

moons revolving around a common sun, Cirincione,
D'Amato, and Ferraro often exchange roles and tasks, while
intuitively sharing a understanding of the eventual goal.

Cirincione is a curator and critic deeply committed to
supporting fresh art and ideas and to having the great talent
of artists not languish inside museums and galleries. She is
part of a generation of critics that recognizes the power
harnessed by technology and believes artists, writers, and
poets should be shaping the message and means of that
power before it's too late. Part of her interest in games and
technology is based on a desire to encourage art to exist
beyond institutional confines. Powerfully tenacious, she is
frequently the producer of the group, moving the process
along. D'Amato is a visual and literary artist whose endeavors in each form result from a process of cross-pollination.
His first novel, *Beauty*, is a psychological thriller that co-opts
cosmetic surgery and the pretenses of the New York art
world. His interests stretch over vast territories—Mayan
mythologies, the writings of Roland Barthes, the history of
games, underground comics—to which D'Amato in part
attributes his fascination with interactivity. The ability of
digital technologies to compress and reproduce a myriad of
images and ideas responds to his personal breadth of interests. The painter of the group, D'Amato often creates by
hand the sketches that will then be digitally transformed as
the visual component of the game. However, for Softworlds'
projects, these sketches are based on discussions among the
three. Ferraro is currently a partner of Blue Sky Productions.
His early projects were as a sculptor during the 1970s, when
interactive electronic environments were clumsy and unpre-
dictable—giant main-frame computers hooked up with
miles of cable and duct tape. But it was also a period that
generated much excitement through dreaming up the vast
possibilities. And now, twenty years later, for Ferraro and
others, there finally exists the refined technology with which
to realize those dreams. While much of the technological
detail does fall to Ferraro, he is more preoccupied with the
aesthetic and conceptual structures of the games and the
intellectual meaning expressed by their architecture.

The selection of Softworlds, Inc. for the Wexner Center's
1994 artists residency program in exhibitions was in response

to many of the above-mentioned issues and to a confluence
of apparent resources, initiatives, and ideas among the
artists, the Wexner Center, and The Ohio State University.
In part, the project stemmed from this curator's simple
curiosity about this nexus of art and tech, knowing there
were talented artists—Jenny Holzer, Matt Mullican, Joseph
Nechvetal, and Julia Scher, to name but a few—who were
aggressively exploring this territory. In part, the activities
grew from realizing that the most satisfying of the Wexner
Center's programs are poised at the edge of experimentation,
of testing new initiatives, and that this specific arena had not
been explored in previous programs. In part, the residency
grew in response to the university's resources: the existence
of activity across this campus in digital interfaces and a
student body that is already naturally immersed in technology. And, in part, the residency responded to these three
artists who were ready to create the first full enactment of
their digital art.

The issues and goals addressed by Softworlds are at the
heart of much of the critical discourse surrounding art and
technology. In the broadest perspective, the group strives to
create digital world designs that integrate developing technology with aesthetic content and investigate how the language
of interactivity can serve as a viable artistic medium. Additionally, Softworlds wants to position its current endeavors
and future projects with other collaborators in a realm that is
accessible, that moves beyond conventional art sites and into
existing information systems, networks, and consumer
technologies. This desire goes beyond merely widening the
potential distribution for this work to address a fundamental
and perhaps utopian belief that artists, their work, and their
ideas must be an integral part of the social fabric.

The specific focus of the residency is the creation and
presentation of *Softworld 2.1: The Imperial Message.* Initially
envisioned as an anti-war/interactive game experience, it is
also independent of a specific delivery or presentation
system. This is not merely a practical consideration, responding to the ongoing gap between the promise and the
reality of VR or other evolving technologies, but more
directly addresses the philosophical tenets of Softworlds.
Cirincione, D'Amato, and Ferraro do not aim to exploit the

latest or sexiest digital phenomena. Rather, they aspire to create experiences built upon aesthetic and contextual concerns that are new to the digital world. *Sacrifice,* their first project, and *The Imperial Message* are both based on board games: Parchessi and go, respectively. Utilizing the mythology and structure of games enables the artists to communicate in a commonly understood language and to exploit the metaphoric content of games: Parchessi is essentially a religious model of the universe; go is a strategy for conquering territories.

Perhaps most critically, the game experience defines a specific sense of place. The propensity to reinvent and redefine notions of place, whether in a digital world or in an artist's imagination, is among the most compelling challenges confronting us today. Our collective understanding of place must be continually revised amid the onslaught of electronic and scientific advancements. This is why the concept of cyberspace is both so frightening and so exhilarating: it radically reconfigures what and where place can be, its physicality, its temporality. The game structure itself then becomes a new medium. Softworlds is not interested in duplicating the laws of physics in virtual spaces, but rather in exploiting those rules. Interactivity and games also enable the artists to examine such topics as control versus passivity and how truly "mediated" interaction is. By manipulating architectural and theatrical systems, and scripting narratives that branch infinitely, they can further investigate the implications—artistic and ethical—of creating worlds… even if they are *soft.*

Sarah J. Rogers, *Director of Exhibitions*

Art, Wisdom, and Purpose

Perhaps the easiest, and yet most telling, question artists can be asked about their work is "What is your purpose?" Assumptions about the purposes and functions of artmaking, or, indeed, any fabricating activity, have changed over time. In the most recent past, at least in the Western cultural tradition, we have witnessed the making of art based on aims that work both toward and against equating aesthetics with values outside the world of art.

Asking the question "What is your purpose?" of artists working with virtual technologies might then inherently include questions about the purposes and functions employed to develop that technology, since virtual systems were originally developed not for artistic purposes, but for military ones. In using virtual technologies for artmaking, are artists accepting or rejecting those initial developmental assumptions? In order to answer that question, it is helpful to clarify the assumptions associated with current virtual system development and the origins of those assumptions.

Two themes consistently emerge in writings about virtual reality: simulation and artificial reality.[1] Both of these themes are technological priorities that can be traced directly to the end of the sixteenth century and the beginning of the seventeenth, when Kepler, Bacon, and then Descartes set an artificial and unreachable limit for knowledge specifically undertaken to advance the possibility of modern science. The effect of setting this limit was the separation of moral and intellectual spheres, and the repercussions of that separation remain evident in every aspect of Western culture. The misplaced need for epistemic certainty has been reinforced by the designing of machines that obligingly fill this need, and we have placed our confidence in those machines and their qualities: efficiency, speed, objectivity, measurement, and innovation for its own sake. This list of qualities does not describe the full range of human capabilities, and the emphasis on them to the exclusion of other characteristics has helped to erode our faith in human judgment and human worth.

1. See, for example, Brenda Laurel, *Computers as Theatre* (Reading MA: Addison-Wesley, 1991); Howard Rheingold, *Virtual Reality* (New York: Summit Books, 1991); Allucquere Rosanne Stone, "Will the Real Body Please Stand Up?: Boundary Stories about Virtual Cultures," in Michael Benedikt, ed., *Cyberspace: First Steps* (Cambridge MA: MIT Press, 1991), pp. 81–118); and Benjamin Woolley, *Virtual Worlds: A Journey in Hype and Hyperreality* (Cambridge MA: Blackwell Publishers, 1992).

In working with and becoming involved in the aesthetic development of virtual systems, artists are either accepting or rejecting, stabilizing or altering, assumptions about the necessity of human judgment and human worth. As artists make aesthetic choices, they suppose certain ideas about the purposes and values of artmaking. These ideas have changed over time and have come from various sources, both internal and external to the artmaking process, but they have had primary impact on what was communicated by and about the art of any particular time. Ethics and aesthetics both can be defined in terms of judgment. It is this partnership that allows us to grapple conceptually with both areas of thought at once. But it is their active involvement in the artmaking process that will allow us to understand the consequences of that partnership. The separation of moral and intellectual thought described above has had enormous influence on judgment involved in both ethics and aesthetics.

Kant's outline of the characteristics of aesthetic judgment in his *Critique of Judgment*, considered a direct descendent of Cartesian philosophy, has been the most influential underlying aesthetic philosophy since its conception during the nineteenth century. Contemporary changes in aesthetic philosophy, intricately linked to corresponding changes in epistemology and ethics, have centered around questions of the objectivity of judgment in these areas of thought. From the "disinterested" withdrawal from political, social, and moral considerations that characterized the Kantian aesthetic, aesthetic judgment moved through a period of relativism in which the objectivity of judgment, the values on which judgments were based, and the identities of those who made judgments were taken into serious consideration. More recently, an understanding of what is provided by the essential link of judgment between knowledge, aesthetics, and ethical choice has emerged from this period of relativism. This understanding has provided practitioners in all three areas with the possibility of seeing wisdom as a goal, if we define wisdom as "not just to talk about the world, or to be informed about it, but to act rightly in it," as philosopher of ethics Mary Midgley puts it.[2]

If we now come back to our interest in the purposes and functions of artists' involvement with virtual technologies,

2. Mary Midgley, *Wisdom, Information and Wonder: What is Knowledge For?* (London: Routledge, 1989), p. 21.

we are able to clearly recognize the tenacity with which the question "What is your purpose?" clings to artistic exploration of such technologies. The beginning of an answer to that question is that it is not enough just to make art about virtual reality, or to be informed about it. Artists' engagement with a virtual system inherently involves decisions about how to act rightly in it. The acquisition of knowledge that will enable artists to work with already developed virtual systems is important, as are understanding and communicating the consequences inherent in doing so. Choosing to accept or revise those systems, however, is the crucial component in finding an answer to the question of purpose.

How to redefine virtual systems is a more difficult question, if only because an essential component of those systems, interactivity, is an aesthetic, ethical, and epistemological consideration little understood in or pertinent to the dominating aesthetic of the last century. To make art that takes on the responsibility of choosing how to act in the world, and consequently, takes on the responsibility of aiming at wisdom, the artist cannot help but eventually realize that the making of wisdom—the making of a wise choice—is not possible without the input of others.

Softworlds' choice of a Kafka parable as a touchstone for the group's explorations of virtual systems is revealing for this reason. Alice Miller, a noted psychoanalyst, makes a strong case for the origination of Kafka's writings in his childhood psychological abuse. If one looks in general at the situation of an adult whose childhood suffering is inaccessible to him, and was caused by a mother who not only did not understand the child, but did not notice him, we may see its connection to a writer whose entire body of work is permeated with "the tragedy of never making any headway with even the simplest, most logical ideas and always running into stone walls."[3]

The point Miller makes for the individual, as well as for society as a whole, is that to only substitute one hierarchy of control or authority for another is useless, and ultimately defeating to the goal of maturation. We must fully understand the truth of the originating situation in order to escape or change what is devastating to our growth as an individual, or to our growth as a society.

3. Alice Miller, *Thou Shalt Not Be Aware: Society's Betrayal of the Child*, American ed., trans. Hildegarde and Hunter Hannum (New York: Farrar, Straus, Giroux, 1984), p. 261.

In the same way for artists working with virtual systems, merely substituting one aesthetic hierarchy for another is ultimately self-defeating. Replacing the hierarchy of an aesthetic developed out of the requirements of the military with an aesthetic that has developed out of an art world concerned with the exigencies of losing its privileges as the purveyor of "artistic truth" will not allow or encourage what Michael Benedikt, in his essay in this volume, describes as "a public good." Virtual systems can only be developed as a public good if the aesthetic under which they are developed includes all segments of that public as essential participants, and sees the purposes and functions of artmaking as intricately bound up with a wisdom that emerges from a compassionate concern for the needs of that public.

Carol Gigliotti, *Education and Technology Liaison*
and *Assistant Professor, Department of Art Education*

*If you only followed the parables you yourselves would become
parables and with that rid of all your daily cares.*
Another said: I bet that is also a parable.
The first said: You have won.
The second said: But unfortunately only in parable.
The first said: No, in reality: in parable you have lost.[1]

—Franz Kafka, "On Parables"

Overview: Sacrifice and The Imperial Message

In digital world experiences, simulation, abstraction, realism, point of view, and control can potentially bridge the schisms between reality and parable. What lessons can we learn within these imaginary realms that at once mimic and shroud physical reality? How can these technological places strengthen our experience of "real" space? Softworlds' approach to making art and play through digital designs begins to address these questions.

Softworlds' initial project, *Softworld 1.2: Sacrifice,* is a template of the group's overall interests. Text and images (most static, some animated) are orchestrated into a succession of potential adventures. Both words and pictures articulate an atmosphere that is evocative and carefully crafted, as in an illustrated novel. And as in an arcade game, the play is goal-oriented and set in a rigidly circumscribed place controlled by specific laws and myths. The objective of *Sacrifice* is to "kill" yourself as often and as spectacularly as possible so that you are reincarnated into progressively advanced zones of the landscape, arriving, if you kill yourself often enough, at the "Heart of the Sky." In typical arcade games, the player strives to avoid death—although reincarnation is possible by inserting another coin and beginning again, only to repeat a similar journey. In this way, the structure of the Softworlds game ironically underscores the singularity of commercial games and their simplistic and stridently dichotomous social order: you win, you lose/ you live, you die/you're good, you're bad. *Sacrifice* complicates these rules by encouraging the player to die (in dramatic and noble ways, of course) in the pursuit of the proper path of sacrifice that will eventually lead to a winner's circle in the glorious Heart of the Sky. Even the concept of nobility (at least as presented in arcade games) is perverted by Softworlds: in the controversial game *Mortal Kombat,* it is noble to beat one's opponent bloody and senseless; in *Sacrifice,* it is noble to destroy oneself in pursuit of the goal—to win by dying a hero.

BY SARAH J. ROGERS

1. Franz Kafka, "On Parables," in *Parables and Paradoxes,* (New York: Schocken Books, 1975), p. 11.

Softworlds investigates new technologies and new art forms derived from those technologies. We question how to apply artistic practices to technology. The goal is to come up with products of a higher standard than these technologies are normally used for.

The scenic architecture of the game is an expansive terrain that looks and functions like the game board for chess or Parcheesi. From a panoramic point of view at the beginning of the game, territories and limits are laid out before the player. The scene is at once other-worldly and familiar: a modernist, ziggurat-shaped temple that is called the Citadel; an exquisitely rendered pink sky recalling dramatic coastal sunsets. The terrain appears vast, its scale dwarfing any sense of human proportion. At the same time, the austerity of the scene beckons one closer to see what might exist inside the ominous structure. The Citadel recalls the temple mounds or artificial mountains (known as *mulob*) clustered in the center of Mayan cities. In *Sacrifice* the temple precinct contains separate quadrants—the Jaguar House, the Bat House—in which an adventurous player encounters canyons with rivers of pus, an onyx bat chamber, a moon woman. These places and characters are fanciful inventions by Softworlds, loosely based on specific Mayan symbols. Questions are posed to the player, who responds by deciding which direction to take. The choices are sometimes fatal and noble, other times cowardly and hollow.

By drawing upon pre-Columbian Mayan culture as an aesthetic and mythological resource, Softworlds adeptly condenses gaming strategies with a desire to explore the evocative power of constructed worlds. The mythology provides a ready-made vocabulary and aesthetic from which to work and taps into archetypal images of control, power, good, and evil that are the conceptual underpinnings of most games. The exterior, introductory scenes are computer-generated graphics; the interior scenes are digitized watercolors by Brian D'Amato. The inclusion of pictures that retain their painterly, handmade appearance even after digital processing negates the technological, sci-fi quality and expresses a more mysterious, dreamlike character. This is perhaps a subtle distinction, but one that clearly distinguishes Softworlds' art. The group is actively seeking a new description of place in a digital world. Not content to rework current digital topographies—a futuristic world that looks feudal and is populated by gladiators, ninjis, or medieval warriors—Softworlds hopes to mine what can be universally understood in such stereotypes, but then manipulates and perverts those concepts into expressive forms.

The specific selection of ancient Mayan culture as source also stems from the artists' desire to exploit issues of colonialism (cultural and territorial), of victimization, of human sacrifice (psychological as well as physical), and of control. These topics refer specifically to the period in history when Central America was colonized by Europeans, when indigenous peoples lost control of their destiny. Similar fears are expressed today in relation to interactivity and technology. Who is being colonized? How are we being controlled? Is the player a victim or a hero? Will only the privileged have access to these new conditions?

The experience of *Sacrifice* is playful and engages the basic human desire to defeat one's opponent. Even the initially passive player is quickly taken over by the anxious desire to experience the worst threat and emerge victorious. The nature of this play also sketches out critical territories that Softworlds will pursue in future work—issues of control and the impact of technology upon daily behavior—drawing our attention (even when at play and perhaps our guard is down) to the individual's changing relationship to the world: physical, technological, social, psychological, and aesthetic. Who and what are to be sacrificed?

Softworld 2.1: The Imperial Message charts several courses in search of possible answers to such questions. The project was originally conceived as an anti-war game inspired by Franz Kafka's parables and the artists' readings about imperial China. As it evolved, *The Imperial Message* incorporated critiques of both games and actual historical precedents that glorify war and colonization or pit individuals against their communities.

Again, the artists have designed a game to be played individually: you are both protagonist and opponent; you encounter various characters and make choices as you attempt to navigate through a city in search of "the Source of the Law" personified by "the Emperor." The Kafka parable *An Imperial Message* describes the distance between ruler and subjects: a servant is given a message by a dying emperor and sent to deliver it beyond the city gates. The messenger of the parable soon learns it is an endless journey, and that he can never deliver the message. Softworlds' game is not an illustration of the parable, but it is inspired by the dilemmas Kafka's story presents: conflicts between loyalty and responsibility, original intent and practical manifestation, idealized and practical truths.

The game is constructed around several inherent strategies. The architecture of the game is hierarchical and not labyrinthine: this is expressed in the type of programming language, which routes the players through different branches of the game, as well as in the "physical" features of this imaginary landscape and its buildings. At the very beginning of the game, the player is captured and confronted by several guides who set the scene. Next the player confronts three inquisitors who ask several pointed questions ("Would you sacrifice your family for the Emperor? Could you assassinate the Emperor and take over rule yourself?"). The answers to these questions establish a "prisoner profile" of the player's character traits, such as his/her relationship to authority, and then determine the player's destiny: play is individuated by response. As the various paths are opened, players may confront a vast gridded plain that resembles a go board punctuated by hut-like structures (based on the design of Siberian yurts), interior rooms that reveal themselves like a series of "Chinese boxes," a grand palace whose interior is a vast panopticon, a tiny blue pyramid inside of which is an infinite world covering the entire planet. Such structures are constructed by integrating real-time CGI simulation, sophisticated proprietary software, programs based on deductive reasoning and artificial intelligence, and role-playing game strategies originally developed for military simulations. This structural collage of software systems generates a world that possesses its own unique rules. *The Imperial Message* engenders a pictorial and social structure as metaphor for the "real world."

But what does such a world look like? How are the aesthetic choices made by Softworlds distinctive? In part the beauty of this digital empire is indebted to the artists' understanding of the highly sophisticated software. And in part, it is indebted to the delicacy with which architectural structure and form are mapped and conceived in relation to the details of color, light, and atmosphere. Each component is designed as a fusion of its content, purpose, and structure. This is most strikingly accomplished in the overall view of the empire. At the beginning of the game, we are told, "You have been accused of free-thinking." What we see is an expansive fortress that begins at the tip of a spiral and then radiates out into a sprawling structure that appears increasingly complex and unstructured. This seemingly spontaneous growth, this unraveling of an ordered form into less-ordered states, conveys visual and symbolic entropy. As entropy in the sciences measures the disorder of a system, the metaphoric entropy in *The Imperial Message* measures the inevitable disintegration of societal orders. It is a momentum in which the player is trapped—the force of destiny draws you through the game by a "systolic imperative," as Michael Ferraro describes it.[2] This visual momentum is accentuated by the series of musical compositions by Alvin Lucier. Loosely based on Lucier's early works, this score is minimal, often played with only a single instrument and acoustic. The subtle tonal values highlight a dramatic moment of play or mark a shift in mood.

So far, the aspects of *The Imperial Message* have been described with no mention of the hardware through which the software will be presented. This is because for Softworlds the presentational or "delivery" system is secondary to the content. The artists are not seduced by the "gee-whiz" effects of technology—although they do share a healthy fascination with such great treats as high-density monitors and 3-D projection cubes. Softworlds sees such inventions as changing more rapidly than the programs to utilize them can be created. Such an approach gives the artists and their programs the flexibility to adapt to such changes. At the Wexner Center, *The Imperial Message* will be experienced in a feedback immersion helmet and through a configuration of three video projection cubes where play is controlled by a joy-stick so that individual play can be witnessed by those gathered around the screens. *Sacrifice* will be available in a separate part of the gallery, played on a touch-screen and viewed on a projection cube.

Repeated play of the *The Imperial Message* will reveal additional issues that the artists are exploring: from gender to the physical imposition of VR and general expectations about interactivity. Although the artists describe their carefully

2. It is interesting to note that in the Kafka parable the description of the scene at the Emperor's death also signals an entropic condition, physically and emotionally: "Yes, before the assembled spectators of his death—all the obstructing walls have been broken down…" See Kafka, "An Imperial Message," in *Parables and Paradoxes*, p. 13.

designed world as "genderless," it is difficult to ignore what at first seem to be clichéd role assignments. The Emperor is a male and dominates an explicitly patriarchal society. The guides and messengers are androgynous, but their voices and movements are implicitly feminine. While the game equates the Emperor with the Source of the Law, Softworlds also empowers these other characters with the power of information. Perhaps in this way the artists are subtly subverting the hierarchy of the adolescent-male-fantasy game world—controlled by powerful men—in their imperial universe.

The evocative and symbolic ways Softworlds manipulates scale within the scenes address both the physical experience of the player and the larger notion of interactivity. In part the drama of the game is achieved through the distortions of scale as the player moves through the landscapes. The odd hybrid of naturalistic atmospheres and fantastic buildings is disorienting and transformative—and recalls the way Lewis Carroll masterfully moves the reader down the rabbit hole into Wonderland. Such visual distortions are underscored and enhanced by the manner in which the game impacts us physically. When using the immersive head-gear to wander these digital terrains, the body literally becomes an extension of a machine. It is an "unnatural," awkward imposition and provokes questions as to how such mechanization of the human anatomy might redefine our self-perceptions.

The experience of *The Imperial Message* leads us to an important observation: interactivity is not an unmediated experience. In fact it is carefully controlled and the parameters of choice are quite narrow. In this game, the player is trapped in a universe where cause and effect are largely predetermined but where the individual is required to exercise some control. In broader terms, the game is self-reflective with respect to the general role of technology in our daily lives: isn't the seemingly vast and impenetrable nature of a technology that is forbidden, yet desired, not unlike the Emperor? This technology also must be examined in relationship to the "real world." How will experiences that can so enhance the senses change (diminish or augment) our perceptions of the natural world? Perhaps most provocative in the context of this nexus of art and tech is the question of imagination and our freedom to dream. Will digital worlds fulfill an innate desire to mingle the real with the imaginary?

Ultimately, *Sacrifice* and *The Imperial Message* simulate certain kinds of journeys that are a search for something unknown or unnamed, an escape from what is known. Digital worlds provide a vehicle for such travels, but it remains the human imagination that defines what and where these journeys will be. In 1974 Italo Calvino wrote an astonishing novel that resonates particularly clearly today as we enter these new realms of technology. *Invisible Cities* describes the interaction between the emperor Kublai Khan and the adventurer Marco Polo, who returns to the emperor with tales of the distant places he has been. The descriptions reveal as much about the human desire to understand a sense of place as they do about specific details of any one place. The narrator observes "Arriving at each new city, the traveler finds again a past of his that he did not know he had: the foreignness of what you no longer are or no longer possess lies in wait for you in foreign, unpossessed places." The tale continues: " 'Journeys to relive your past?' was the Khan's question at this point, a question which could also have been formulated: 'Journeys to recover your future?' And Marco's answer was: 'Elsewhere is a negative mirror. The traveler recognizes the little that is his discovering the much he has not had and will never have.' "[3] So too are the foreign terrains of digital frontiers.

The comments by Softworlds in this section of the catalogue are from interviews Sarah J. Rogers conducted with Janine Cirincione, Brian D'Amato, and Michael Ferraro between January and March 1994.

VR and interactivity are such new media—we're at the stage where there are more possibilities than limitations. When we began this residency we stated that we would be developing the language of interactivity, and we actually seem to be doing that. Since there are no existing standards we have the opportunity to define them.

3. Italo Calvino, *Invisible Cities*, trans. William Weaver (New York: Harcourt Brace & Company, 1974), p. 28–29.

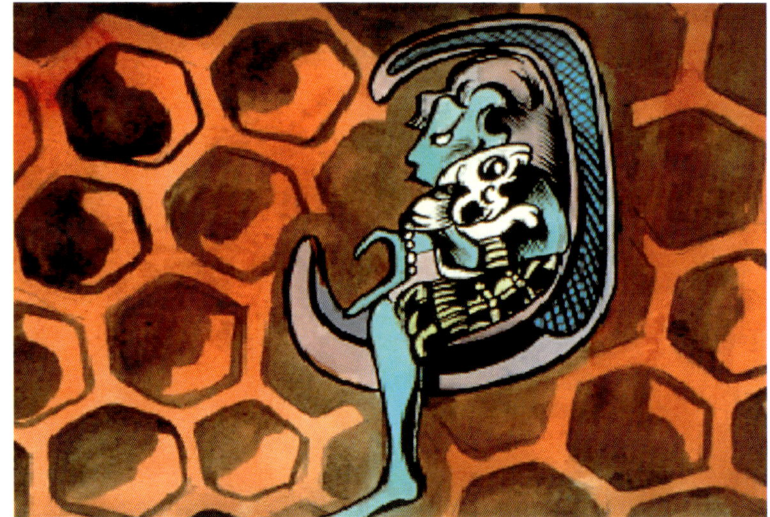

Interactivity has a very long history—low brow and low tech. There are simple theater performances in which participants from the audience form part of the drama. Bruce Nauman has been working with interactivity for many years in a very low-tech way, creating structures that you are forced to interact with and be manipulated by physically, and/or with video scans and projectors. Interactivity is far more complex when it is driven by a computer. Computers are great at structuring narratives which are nonlinear and seemingly infinite. The flexible structure [of the computer] can resemble the way the mind works, looping and searching. But it is important to beware of the hype of interactivity, which sets up the expectation that you can do anything at all. The fact is that you can't.

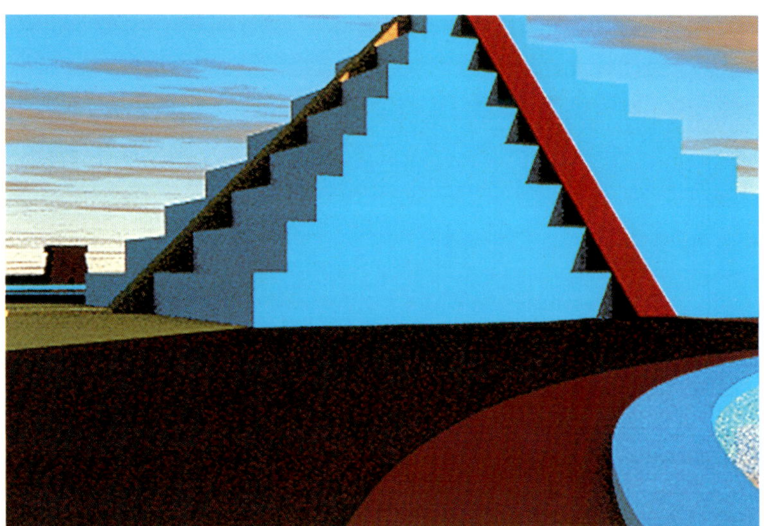

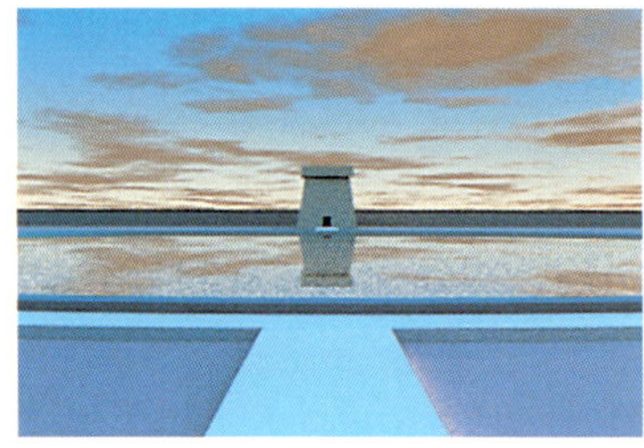

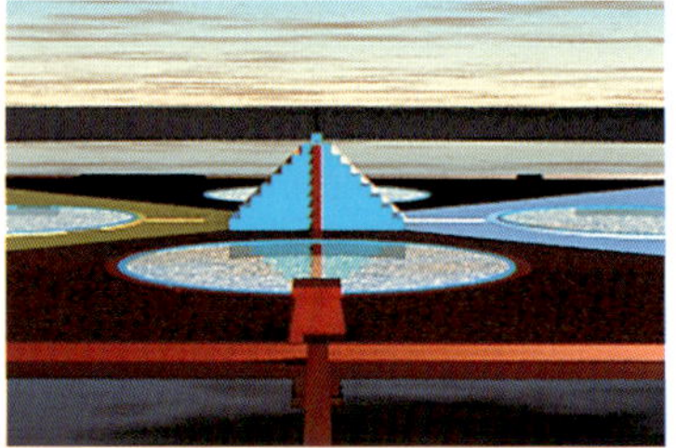

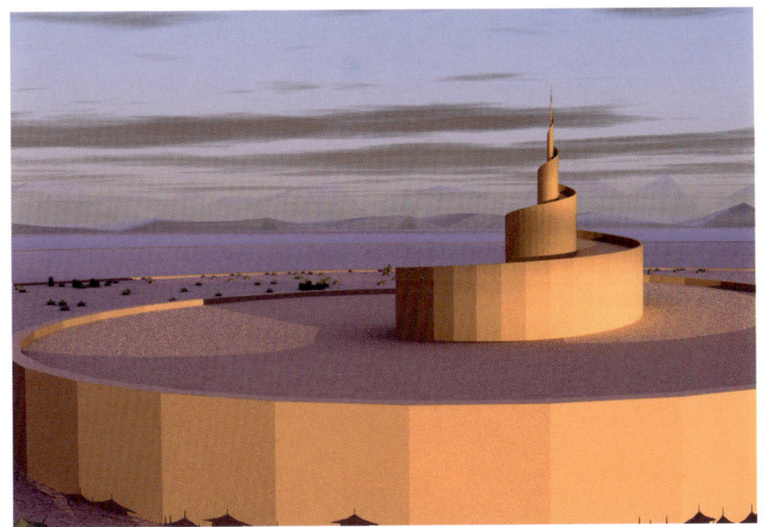

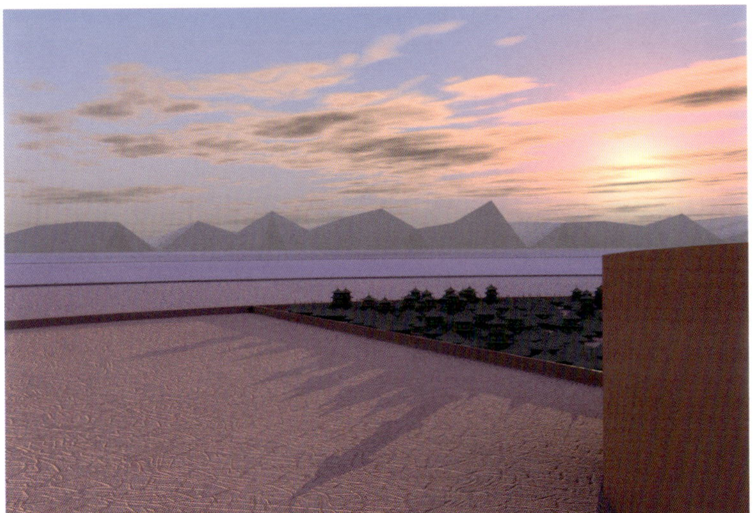

Our work differs from what other people do in interactivity in that we're primarily concerned with content, and a lot of artists tend to focus on the paraphernalia. There tends to be a sort of science-fiction fascination with the cyborgish hardware of current display devices, and we completely avoid that. We don't really want the delivery system—the monitors or the head-mounted displays—to be a feature of the work. It's really about the software, because the delivery systems will change very much over time. We hope that we can create the most memorable worlds or visions, that we can create resonant places for people to spend time in.

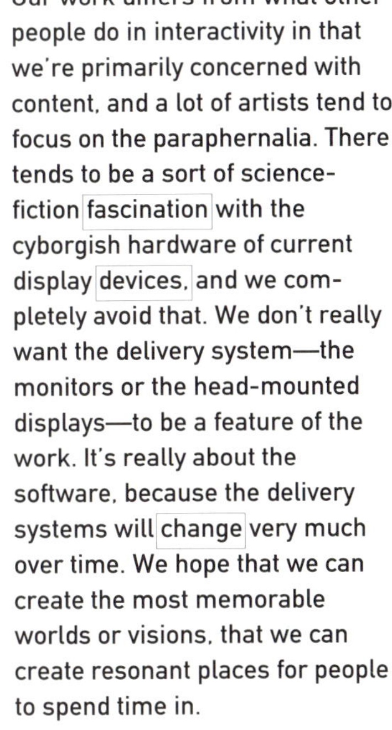

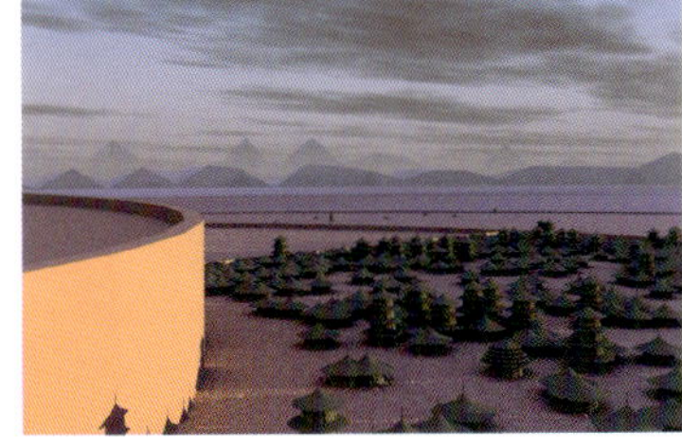

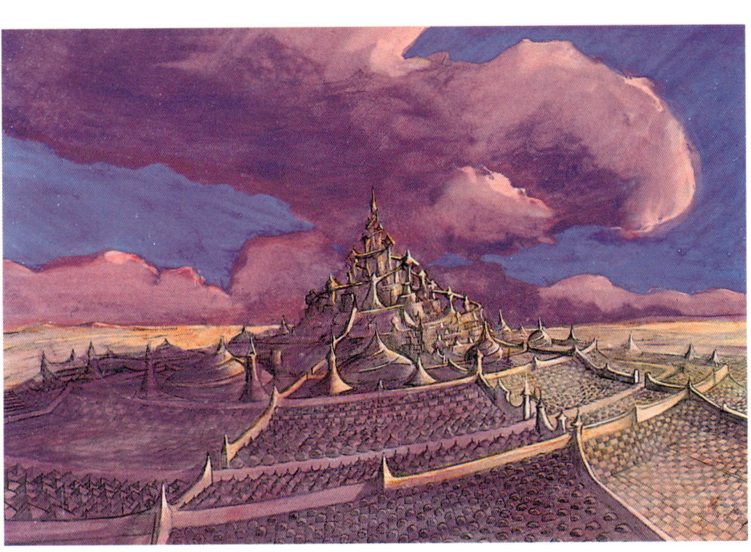

facing page: Stills from *Sacrifice*, 1993

this page: *The Imperial Message*

top: *Spiral*
detail from animated
fly-through, 1994

middle left: *The City and Parapet at Dawn*
detail from animated
fly-through, 1994

middle right: *The City*
detail from animated
fly-through, 1994

bottom: *Set Concept #1*,
pencil and oils on
illustration board, 9/1993

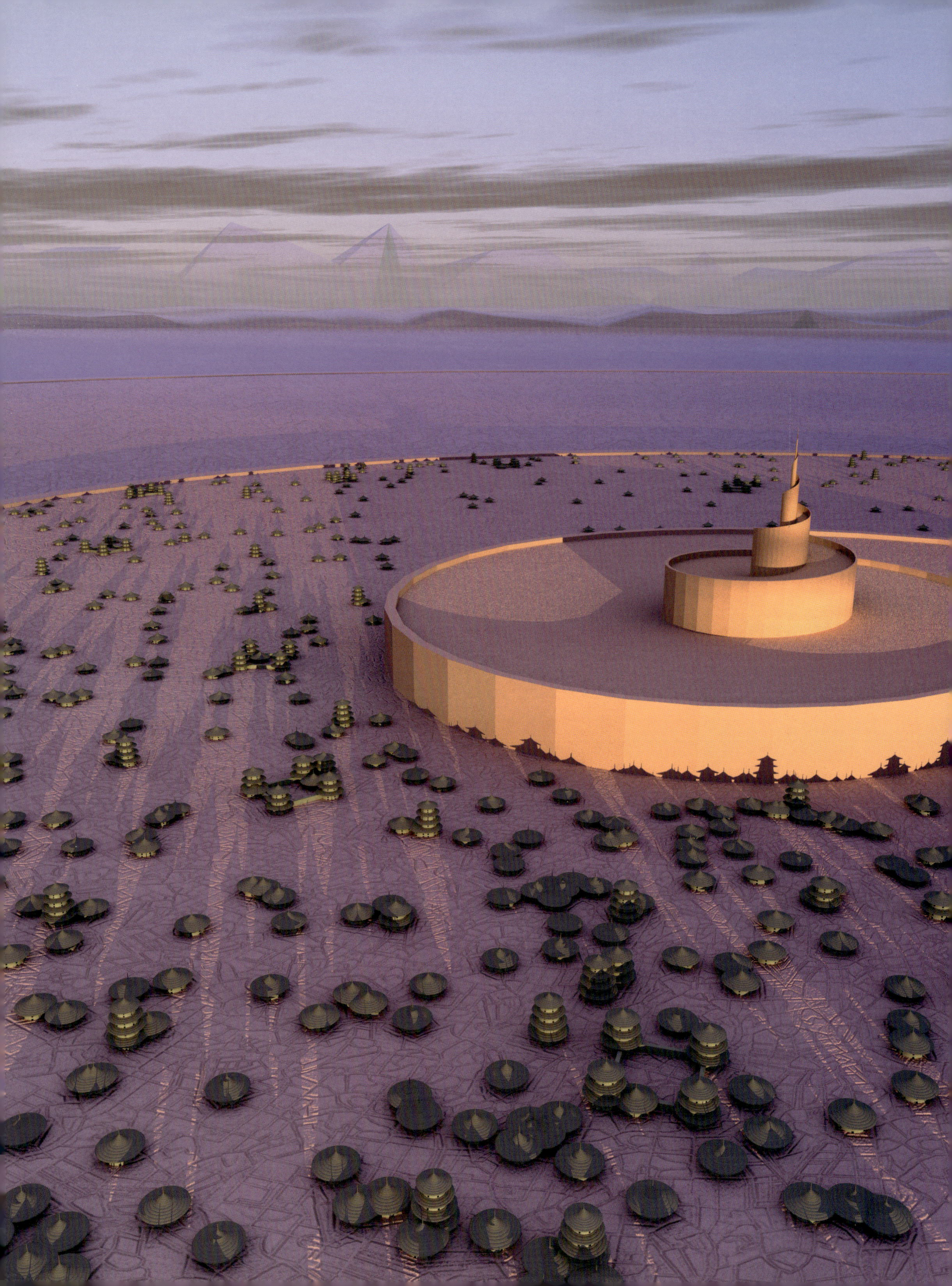

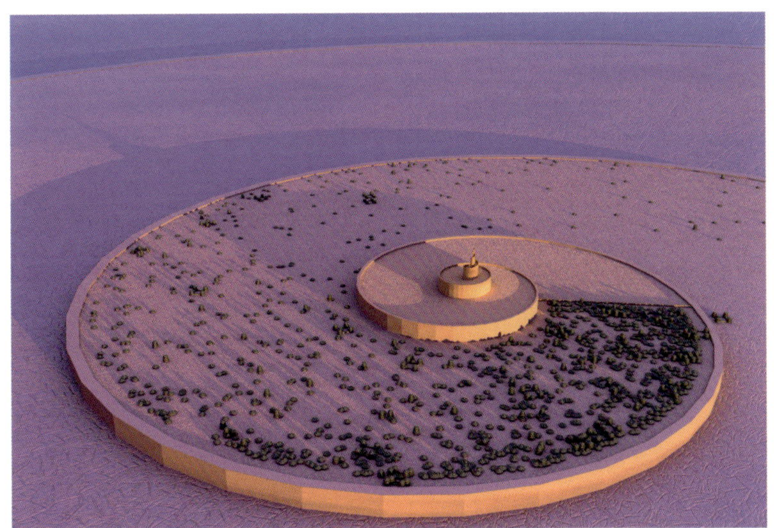

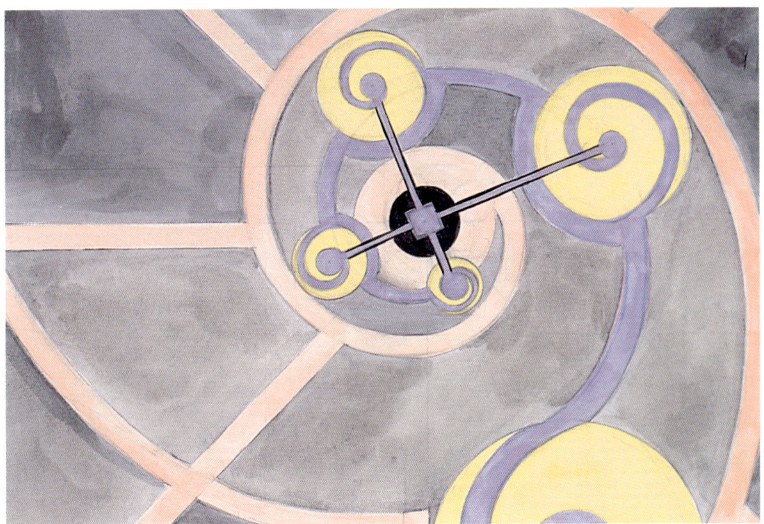

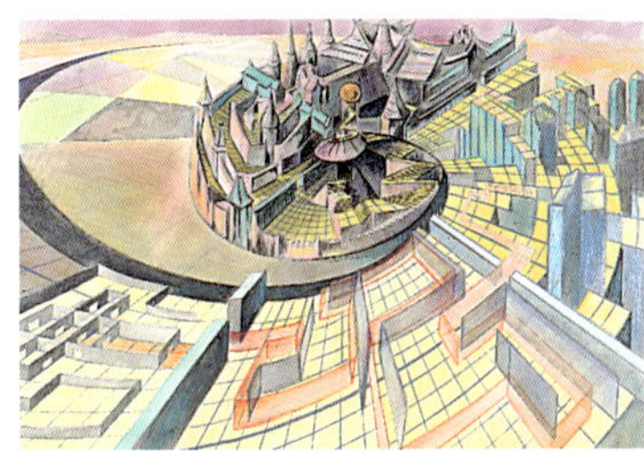

In our work, artistic and aesthetic decisions are the primary driving force. The intention is to have images which are provocative, which are seductive, which hook the intellect through a certain kind of beauty. We're using extremely high quality animation and rendering software to try to add visual richness to the experience, so the pictures by themselves can become beautiful, mysterious, transcendent.

facing page: *The Imperial Message*
The Empire
detail from animated fly-through, 1994

this page: *The Imperial Message*

top: *The Empire* (aerial long view)
model shot, 1994

bottom left: *Set Concept #1: Audience Chamber*
(plan)
watercolor on board, 7/1993

bottom right: *Set Concept #1: Using*
Go-Board Motif
inks and pastel on board, 9/1993

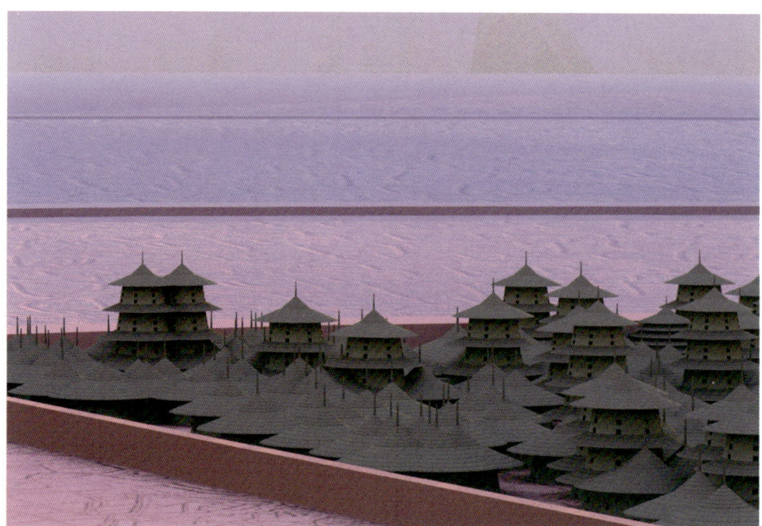

We operate together in the arena of concepts: the metaphor, the content, how it's going to look, the feeling we want evoked, the orchestration of a work in the abstract sense of the term and how those abstract ideas are materialized. The Softworlds organization is three minds spreading the responsibility around and allowing us to develop an objectivity.

32

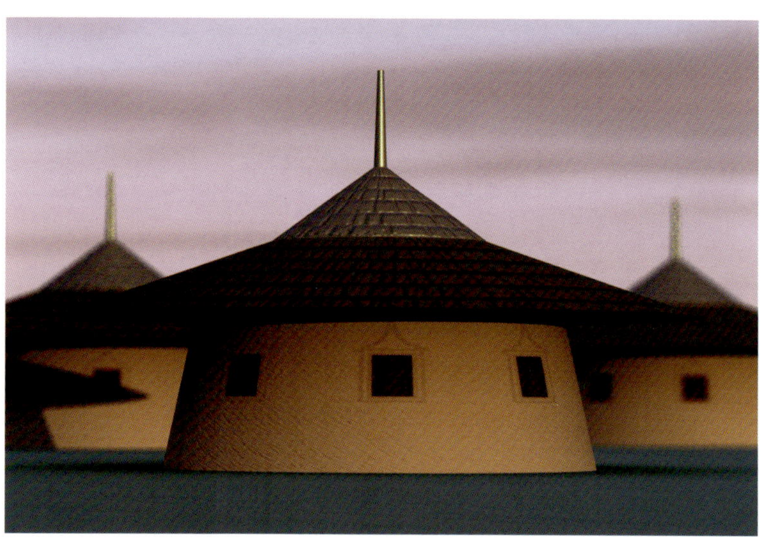

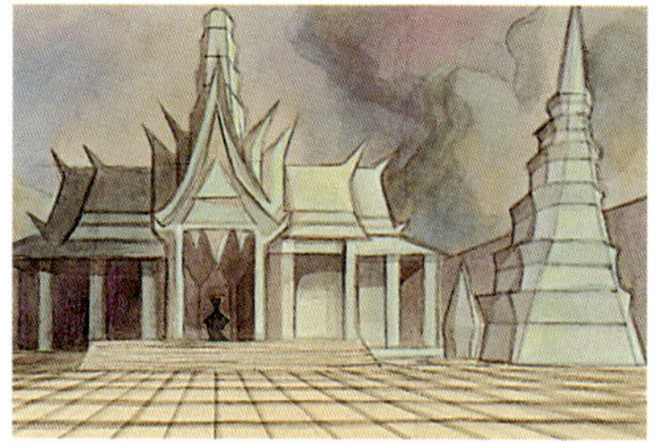

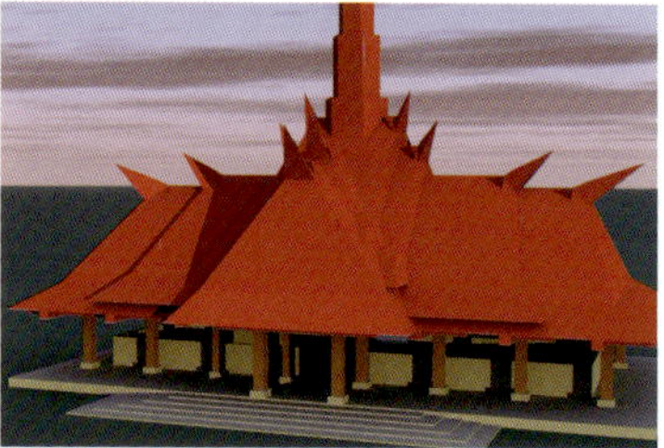

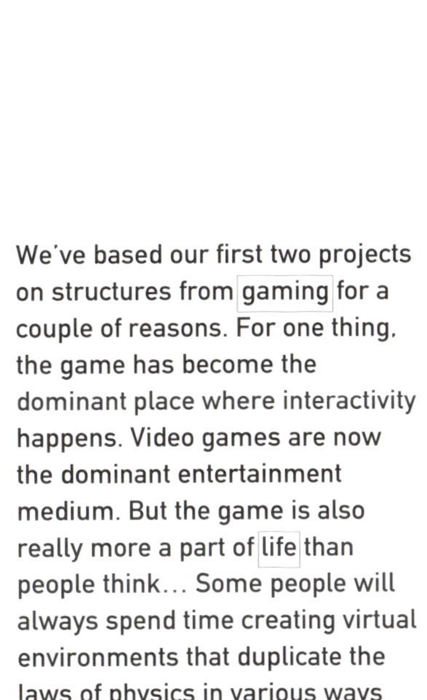

We've based our first two projects on structures from gaming for a couple of reasons. For one thing, the game has become the dominant place where interactivity happens. Video games are now the dominant entertainment medium. But the game is also really more a part of life than people think… Some people will always spend time creating virtual environments that duplicate the laws of physics in various ways that duplicate the real world, but this isn't really that interesting.

What might be more interesting would be to find other structures that provide the kind of difficulty and effort and suffering that people will need in these realms, but which are not so tied to the real world. It seems that if we are to look for sources for these, we would have to look at games… Games are very metaphysical. Certain games are in fact the key components of several cultures. The great games of civilization are tremendously important controlling metaphors.

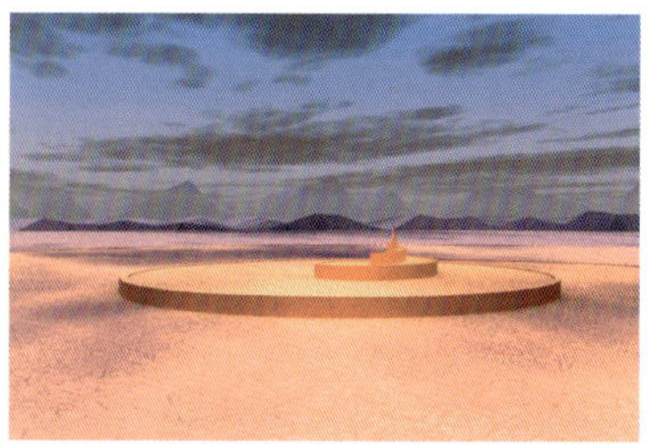 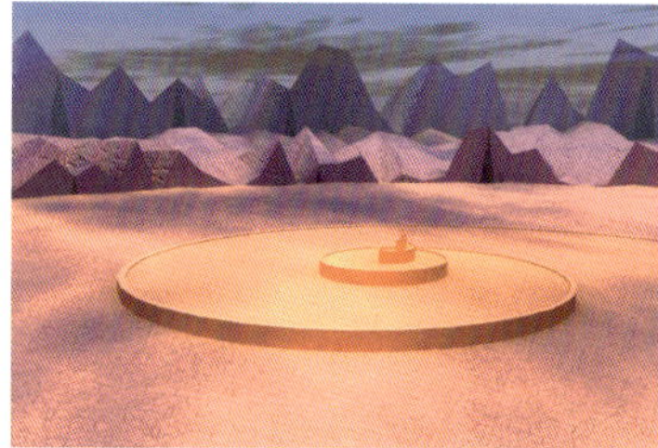 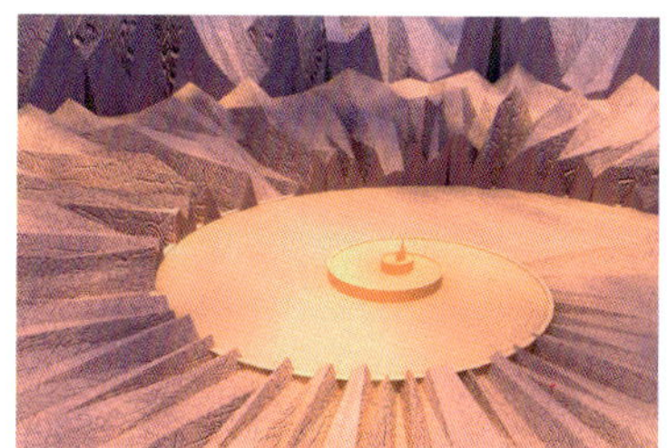

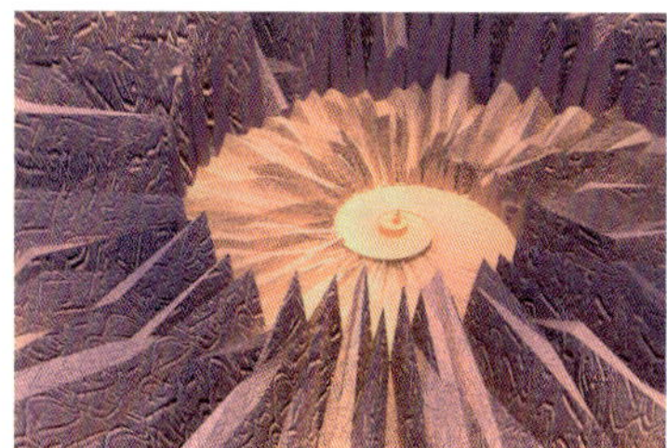 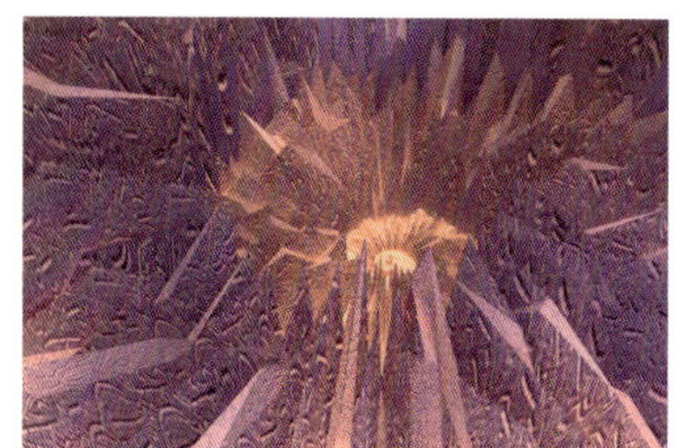

34

The basic structure of a game opens the door to a lot of different things. You can be playful and still introduce powerful ideas in ways that people can discover on their own, through their own meanderings. We've looked at many, many, many video games and [Michael's] looked at computer animation for what seems to be all [his] professional life. We're at a point now where we can make thoughtful choices about why something looks the way it does—the organization of the forms is neither haphazard nor just trying to mimic physical reality. We're making very conscious choices to explore the formal aspects of the shapes, the color, the lighting, the time of day—all the mood aspects that really make the piece a place that you want to be in.

Physics for Phantoms

BY MICHAEL BENEDIKT

This is possible in a virtual world: to pass into the space under a table or in a cabinet or vase, and there discover spaces teeming with life and larger than the room from which they were entered. Within these, in turn, there may be smaller spaces—things with interiors like photo albums or lanterns—which turn out to contain worlds vaster yet… and so on and on, *ad infinitum*, in a Borgesian chain of spaces which grow larger as they are more tightly contained and which may curve back on themselves, so that the final entry into the deepest of deep spaces (no matter which) precipitates us back to where we began, or part of the way back, where we may dive again by another route into inexhaustible innerness. This is a journey through a dimension at once spatial and not; a circle made in an impossible plane; a direction followed which lies at right angles to all others. Is it the fabled *fourth dimension*? Perhaps. For here some Law of Scale is broken the way only children, madmen, and dreamers know it can be.

This too is possible in a virtual world: an object as round and full as a pillow which can be seen through like a window, and this from any and all directions simultaneously. Each viewer who looks through the pillow, whose contour is the shape of the pillow seen in *this* room, sees a pillow-cut view of *another* place, another room, occupying the same space as this one. This pillow/window is nothing more or less than a plump and movable hole, a rotund vacancy, transgressible from all quarters and from both rooms, one into other, back and forth as we please. In our world, the real world, windows have no volume and holes have sides. What Law of Physics is broken here that we might regret?

This too is possible in a virtual world: clouds whose shadows set the earth aflame; chairs that are not chairs but someone in Utah, watching; objects that pass through each other like ghosts or that follow you like the moon; surfaces that can be approached forever but can never be touched, like planets we cannot land on, looming, ever revealing of more detail; a salt shaker which, upon each turn, turns into a figurine, then a tobacco pipe, a crystal log, a hot dog, a laughing bat, a crooked hat, a button-hole maker, and then the salt shaker. Again. Where will the phantasmagoria end? And what is different here from the routine and ritual flauntings of the laws of physics found in fairy tales and Saturday morning cartoons? What is different here that we should take this whole question seriously at all? How important is it that Pacman could disappear on the left of the screen and reappear on the right, or disappear on the bottom to reappear at the top, instantaneously, without it troubling us that the actual *corners* of Pacman's world-surface cannot be joined in any physically realizable topology whatsoever?

One might answer this: there is nothing essentially new in what video games, virtual reality, and cyberspace can show us. Through mythology, folklore, and fiction, through Surrealism and Dada in painting and the movies, through fifty years of commercial art, the ground of the fantastic has largely been covered. Moreover, the fracturing and extension of visual experience under the impact of special effects in cinema, video, and the graphic arts has reached the point where reality itself—streets and trees and buildings, people walking their dogs—has become staid, inherently disappointing, as though caught in a permanent, Sunday afternoon amber. To this stifling familiarity the media bring welcome relief: dislocations and rearrangements, sharpenings of our perception of otherwise just-noticeable differences, "knowledge" of miracles once only read about or heard of.

But, we reply, not for real; never for real. Though we may enter it, Pandora's box remains safely closed. As long as we flip off the switch, take off the helmet, leave the projection room, close the book, get some coffee, go home.

Something else happens, however, when personal virtual worlds *become linked together* and can be shared by many people—by tens, or hundreds, or even thousands of people simultaneously who themselves are located in real places scattered over the globe. This is the vision of *cyberspace*. Suddenly, the closed and marvellous little world of the video game must appear sufficiently similar to all those immersed in it that they can communicate on the basis of what's "really" there, that they can find each other, avoid each other,

and see what others are doing. Such an extended virtual
world must resist transformation. It must be indifferent to
arrivals and departures from it. The *there* we visit must be
there when we return, and when we look back. How strange
that physics should be made necessary by sociality. Who is to
say that this is not already the case?

And something else happens when these virtual worlds are
never turned off, when *life* goes on there whether you witness
it or not, whether you participate in it or not. Games you
cannot afford to leave are not games. When meetings are
held and you are not there, when news is disseminated and
you did not hear, when others more fleet of mind and virtual
of foot plunge deeper and travel further through the glitter-
ing constructs of cyberspace, gathering information, making
deals, and absorbing experiences to their advantage, and
when the whole system grows, as it will, exponentially…
then there will be a penalty for *not* being there. No longer an
amusement, or an art, the finite video game will have become the infinite life game.

It is the boundary between Games and Life that Softworlds
proposes to explore, and it is significant indeed that they
turn to Kafka as others might turn to Borges. In both of
these writers, the Law is carried in the architecture and the
architecture is virtual: capable of a liquidity of scale, of a
dream logic not far from reality but far enough to settle
upon its own faults an air of normalcy. And this is the key:
out-and-out fantasy is easy, the stuff of adolescence. Rationality shattered is not half so compelling as rationality curved
around, sutured. Cyberspace, William Gibson saw, would
begin in video games, and pass through "virtual reality" and
"virtual worlds" on the way. And on the way through them
what was logically possible would shear away from what was
*psycho*logically possible. Likewise, physical law would stand
revealed as the important but *partial* underpinning of social
law that it is. Consider: what is "property" when whole tracts
for new settlement can be fabricated algorithmically and
buried in the eye of a firefly? What is "liberty" when con-
straint upon movement and access to people's consciousness
is governed by neither architecture nor nature, i.e. by neither
gates nor walls nor the fading effects of time and distance,
but by private law: permissions, encryptions, and inabilities

appearing to us as inexplicable lacunae in the data, as silences, circular logics, puzzles, and endless loops? This is defeat by cognitive exhaustion, liberty lost as Kafka prefigured it and only to be re-won, according to Gibson, by the artist/hacker/netrider, keystroke by keystroke.

But is this the only way? It seems to me that in both *Sacrifice* and *The Imperial Message,* Cirincione, D'Amato, and Ferraro of Softworlds explore the critical question of the cognitive and emotional shape of a digital reality. As they have found, when the terrain is swept clean and the air is electrons only, archetypes emerge to fill the vacuum. The power of institutions remains compelling in defining the relation of individual to law as transcribed into space and action, even when inverted. The question as a whole is "critical" because as today's cyberspaces—the space of the telephone, email, MUDs, video-conferences, interactive TV, and on-line data services—coalesce with today's arcade- and museum-grade virtual worlds, logics will emerge that are informed by the reality coded into our bodies: the topo-logic, that is, of four million years of natural evolution as well as the mytho-logic of one hundred thousand years of human cultural evolution, layered upon the topo-logic and constrained by it.

In *Cyberspace: First Steps,* I propose a number of Principles— I hesitated to call them Laws—that might guide the design of cyberspace and virtual worlds, both. These Principles attempt to circumscribe the basis for, rather than describe the details of, cyberspace's "nature," as cyberspace, in turn, manifests human, and evolved, nature. They make, I think, the sort of "good sense" which artists are drawn to test, but defy rendition into easy political critiques.

For example, The Principle of Universal Up states that there needs to be agreement as to which way is "up" in a (multi-user) virtual world, this for two reasons: first that gravitation, though it does not strictly speaking exist in cyberspace, continues to exist in our perceptual apparatus and our expectations of the form of things—any horizontal division of the visual field *is* a horizon, the earth is *below* the sky, things poised on their points or corners topple, and so on. Second, it is likely that *text* will appear in these worlds: signs, banners, documents. Text is orientation-sensitive for its legibility, and so, for that matter, are facial expressions and many, if not most, body gestures. Creators of cyberspaces have control over the direction of virtual gravity, and there are interactions to be considered between this direction and the direction of real gravity (after all, the traveller's body is still here, in a chair) especially when major virtual body movement is involved such as flight, shrinkage, rotation, and braking. Indeed, the larger problem of motion sickness, which is the conflict between optical and inner-ear motion-information to the brain, might never fully be solved.

Here are some of the other Principles. The Principle of Indifference, which we have already touched upon, states that "…the felt realness of any world depends on the degree of its indifference to the presence of a particular 'user' and on its resistance to his/her desire." What is real rather than imaginary always pushes back. Reality always displays a measure of intractability and intransigence. One might even say that "reality" *is* that which displays intractability and intransigence relative to one's personal will. It lies at the intersection of multiple perceptions. This is why what is unreal can rarely generate consensus. The Principle of Indifference also implies strongly that, in a world we take to be real, life goes on in one's absence.

The Principle of Scale states that the maximum velocity of our motion through cyberspace is, and should be, indexed to the (computational) complexity of the world visible around us, including the world that exists behind our back. This introduces a sort of informational inertia or force field which proportions the phenomenological size of a thing with the amount of information it displays. It happens also to con-form to certain computational parameters at the level of hardware.

The Principle of Transit states that "…travel between two points in cyberspace should occur phenomenally through all intervening points, no matter how fast (save with infinite speed), and should incur costs to the traveller pro-portional to some measure of the distance." The idea here is not to succumb entirely to the technology's inherent ability to transport us between remote points in cyberspace instantaneously. For taken to its logical conclusion and finest grain, if we can have instant and motionless "transportation" between any two locations, then we have no space at all. Space—real space or cyberspace—depends on continuity and contiguity in the range of self-movement, and this registering logically with what we can see as possibilities for further movement. Without it, cyberspace becomes, at best, a slide show or video-clip organizer. Moreover, if one is not anywhere when one is "in transport" then opportunities for serendipitous experience are truncated. We become like moles, popping up here and there, and out of sight in between. This question of out-of-sightness brings us to the next Principle, The Principle of Personal Visibility.

The Principle of Personal Visibility is a perfect example of the sort of mixture between two realms of Law, the physical and the social, which the design of virtual worlds and cyberspace forces us to entertain. It states (i) that at all times (when logged in) individual users in/of cyberspace should be *visible*, in some perhaps minimal but never trivial form, to all other users in the vicinity, and (ii) that individual users may choose for their own reasons whether or not, and to what extent, to see/display any or all of the other users in the vicinity. Notice the asymmetry: you may make others invisible to you, but you may not make yourself invisible to others.

Now the first provision of The Principle of Personal Visibil-ity seeks to prohibit individuals from "cloaking" themselves completely in cyberspace. Given the undeniable pleasures—not to say advantages—in real life of seeing but not being seen, of becoming the proverbial "fly on the wall," one wonders why this Principle should carry any weight. Why should the attractions of voyeurism not be allowed to take their "natural" course? (It is estimated, for example, that fully 90% of the "participants" in Internet newsgroups and BBSs are "lurkers": anonymous, invisible, and untrackable readers-only.) I offer two reasons.

The first is essentially political. In any social system founded on contracts and trust, what comes with freedom is *responsi-bility*; and if cyberspace is the "electronic frontier," the site of new freedoms, then it is also, properly and democratically, the site of new responsibilities. Responsibility depends on accountability, and accountability in turn depends on countability, on the obligation, that is, to "stand up and be counted," to be there *to* others if not *for* others. "Hit and run" is what we call action without responsibility. Spying is what we call coming to know without being known to know. A peeping Tom is what we call a person who transgresses our privacy privately. In the physical world, all these actions and modes of presence/non-presence are possible, of course, but difficult. For in the real world we must take our light-reflecting, space-occupying, easily-identifiable, and massy bodies with us. In virtual worlds, however, where our visibility is entirely digitally constituted, these transgressions are easy.

The second reason is less ethically loaded. The presence, number, or spatial disposition of other people in a certain place—not to mention their detailed personal characteristics or actions—constitutes important information in its own right. We learn from the collective actions of others what is good to do, where it is good to be, when it is good to go. We may follow the crowd; we may not. But a world populated only by lurkers would be as empty as a ghost town, like a neutron-bombed Vegas with lights blazing and no visitors… but worse: the night air would have eyes. It flatters architects to imagine how important their structures are *per se*. But to everyone else, *people* matter more: their presence and movement, their appearance and voices. A virtual world consisting of living representations of real people and with a bare minimum of architecture would fare better than a virtual world in which the reverse was the case.

Turning to the second provision of The Principle Personal Visibility shows us the other side of the coin. It says that we ought to be able to screen out, turn off, the sight and sound of others to ourselves. Why? Because we may wish to be alone, to feel alone. A shopping trip, in the real world as in cyberspace, may or may not be enhanced by the experience of the crowds shopping with you. The ability to render others invisible to oneself is an important one, simulating electronically what we do when we close our eyes, draw the curtains, or turn off the phone. But it has political consequences too, ones that we ought to consider. In the real world, people with just and unjust causes can place themselves in public spaces so as to be seen and heard whether we want to or not. They cannot be "screened out," by law. If cyberspace is to have any purely public domains, then, provision (ii) of The Principle of Personal Visibility must be suspended there. And by law.

The subsidized exploration of virtual world and cyberspace technologies by artists—notably at the Banff Center and in the present Softworlds residency at the Wexner Center—marks the beginning of a new phase in the maturation of the Information Age. I say "subsidized," of course, because this is a mode of artistic production that dwarfs most others in terms of the cost of the technology required. No matter how much faster computers become relative to their price, they will not be fast enough to outrun the artistic imagination. Nor will artists be able to afford them. Without the university and public support of artists and architects designing virtual worlds, and without their involvement in the development of cyberspace generally, we shall have what Gibson warned us of: a consciousness-degrading torrent of choiceless choice, kitsch, and commercialism the likes of which has not yet been seen this side of doing acid on Route 10 out of Phoenix. Main-lining TV, Gibson called it. Cyberspace is a public good. Vice President Gore's abandonment of the national "information superhighway" to private development by media conglomerates should give us little hope of realizing a digital world any lovelier than the mall, or Home Shopping Channel, any time soon.

Michael Benedikt is Meadows Foundation Centennial Professor and Director, Center for American Architecture and Design, The University of Texas at Austin.

Someday You'll Be Able to Go to a Party and Be the Only One There: Notes on Virtual Reality

1. A series of isolating techniques has been inextricably linked to the development of industrial society: these techniques have transformed the social over the last 150 years. In the mid-nineteenth century, we can observe the initial curtailment of social intercourse that began in the great European cities: the emergence of the inexpressive, drably uniformed middle-class male as a social type; the replacement of complex rituals of economic exchange in small shops and markets for the silent, fixed-price efficiency of the department store; and the rise of the respectful, ordered, and above all silent audience at the theater and concert hall, trained to react with rigid self-restraint to the virtuosic exaggerations and histrionics of the Romantic performer.

BY PETER HALLEY

Throughout our own century, these regimes of isolation and passivity have intensified. The techniques of the nineteenth century gradually became optimized. The orderliness of the theater has been transformed into the darkness of the cinema, where even applause is unnecessary. The initial anonymity of the department store has developed into McDonald's multiple-choices, computer-screen banking, and the Home Shopping Network. In this century, settlement patterns have also undergone a process of rapid and profound transformation (starting in the last century with the Haussmanization of Paris). The cacophonous heterogeneity of the early modern city, which as much as any other factor gave rise to the ideologies of modernity, has gradually been replaced by the homogeneous, intensely isolating experiences of suburbia, in particular the cloistered world of the detached suburban "home" and the near complete, though complex, aloneness of the suburban automobile. Face-to-face communication was replaced by a sequence of electronic substitutes: first the telephone, then radio, devices for recorded music, television, and most recently the computer terminal.

The net result of these changes is two-fold: first, human beings in this environment live in far greater physical isolation than in the preindustrial or recent past. Real, face-to-face human contact has become minimized (and, when it exists, it is controlled); it is replaced by a medley of placebos that emphatically reflect the logic informing their technological origins. Second, the resulting world is almost completely homogeneous and predictable, devoid of class or ethnic friction, the accidents of chance human encounters, or the irreducible complexity characteristic of more traditional urban patterns.

It is impossible to understand the current popular fascination for the phenomenon of Virtual Reality without taking into account this transformation of the social landscape. The idea of Virtual Reality is an idealized locus for the perfection of this isolating impulse. In Virtual Reality, the individual's isolation becomes finally complete: all his or her perceptual interactions are fulfilled by computer-generated simulacra. In Virtual Reality, the goal of isolating the individual and disenfranchising him or her from all contact with the "real" unmediated perceptual world, and by extension, the unmediated social world, is achieved.

2. One of the most interesting aspects of the Virtual Reality phenomenon, and of computer-generated imagery in general, is the fascination that exists for the computer's ability to reproduce images and visual experiences that duplicate the "naturalistic" world. Thus, for example the idea that computers can reproduce the visual complexity of cloud formations or mountain ranges, through the application of fractal equations, impresses people incredibly. Similarly, the idea that a Virtual Reality "rig" can simulate the spatial experience of flying or falling rapidly though the air creates the same extreme excitement. Several ideologies seem to coalesce to give these visual-spatial experiences their broad appeal.

First, we are drawn in by the ability of the computer to mimic or simulate the natural. We feel a sense of triumph—the triumph of Cartesian reason over the complexity and indeterminacy of "nature." We rejoice that the ordinal processes of the computer can not only store and process information from the human universe, but can seem to reach out to mimic and reproduce the "natural world" as well. There is an ultimate sense of the control of the techno-

logical order over the natural, no less than in nuclear physics
or genetic engineering. It confirms our growing belief that
computers are all-powerful machines whose potential for
mastery is limitless. We are confident that their power can
match if not surpass the power of the physical world in all its
spatio-temporal complexity—and even the power of life
itself.

It should be remembered that Virtual Reality started as a
military technology, intended in particular to simulate
dangerous physical experiences, such as aeronautic dog-
fights, without actual threat to the participants. This chal-
lenge to Thanatos seems to have a particular appeal as
Virtual Reality moves into the realm of popular culture.
(Softworlds' project *Sacrifice* deals with this theme.) The
fictitious enactment of death and violence seems to have a
wide-spread appeal in masculinist cultures in a broad range
of cultural settings. Virtual Reality, as a new standard of
visual "realism," has taken on the role of enacting this as well
as other masculinist fantasies in our current culture. This in
turn raises the question: to what extent is Virtual Reality a
masculinist cultural manifestation? Are the uses to which it
is currently being put specifically masculinist? And the uses
that are envisioned by its visionary fantasists?

Lastly, I believe Virtual Reality currently plays such a visible
role in the present technological-cultural landscape because
it embodies a current tension between two crucial cultural
constructs. Most cultural analysts describe the social universe
that has existed in the West since the Enlightenment as a
realm in which the themes of reason and logic have ruled.
Reason and logic have been the measures by which truth is
tested in Western culture. This investment in reason and
logic has, in turn, resulted in the development of science and
technology. However, despite the current unsurpassed
hegemonic power of technology in our society, there is
reason to believe that, in an important ideological shift, our
culture has begun to turn its back on reason and logic as
cultural truth-measures: that it has begun to return to
images, imagination, and fantasy—the metaphorical truth-
tools of traditional and archaic cultures—as its own measures of forming truth. When recent cultural commentators
lament that we live in a society of "image" and "spectacle,"

they fail to acknowledge their own prejudice in favor of ratio-logical thought that may prevent them from accepting an important shift in the cultural paradigm. But what is unique in the contemporary situation, and what is embodied in Virtual Reality, is that while on the level of technique our culture has in no way abandoned its dependence on ratio-logical processes (specifically science and the computer), there is a new melding by which ratio-logic forces are subsumed to the service of a culture of image, fantasy, and even quasi-mythic narratives for truth.

3. The middle-class suburban landscape of the late-twentieth century has its own set of psychological realities. Relationships are atomized—perhaps to an unprecedented extent. Connections are truncated as families move from house to house or town to town. There is almost no more existent public space where people may interact. Contacts between people, even within families, tend to be based on a specific single purpose (work, being neighbors, a recreational activity) rather than a wide network of shared long-term activities or responsibilities. Despite periodic economic upheavals, life within this kind of setting is extraordinarily safe and protected. People move from place to place, or job to job, but always within the same infantilizing plasma of preestablished social structures that negate the need for choices or responsibility. The condominium, the corporate job, and the mall are all always the same; they are fool-proof structures where nothing will go amiss.

With these factors, new parameters of psychological reality have emerged. In the new suburban context, there are few of the checks and balances on psychological reality that characterize more traditional social settings. A wide range of behavior that could be described as extreme, strange, or deviating (without placing any negative judgments by these terms) comes into being. In an environment without social continuity, there is no need to worry about the "reputation" one's activities will engender, since a person has no reputation. In a setting without threats from crime and without real economic responsibility, it isn't necessary to inhibit behavior because of the restraints on the self caused by such pressures. When the popular media describe the American landscape as a place of cults, incestual and abusive sexual practices, and demon-worship, they may in fact be more accurate than such sensationalism would suggest.

I have undertaken this sketch of the psycho-social reality of suburbia, because the psycho-social space of Virtual Reality is also a reflection of this space. Both in theory and practice, many of VR's proponents imagine Virtual Reality as a space of unleashed fantasies, where the restraints necessitated by the physical reality of the "other" finally and completely disappear. Virtual Reality is envisioned as the ultimate narcissistic space, a space where one's psychological imaginings can be made virtually real. In this sense, the space of Virtual Reality also comes very close to the space of psychosis. The psychotic projects his or her imaginings as real, as hallucinated reality; Virtual Reality's proponents express a yearning for this same kind of hallucinated space.

Interestingly enough, while Virtual Reality's potential for realizing such complete fantasy is not even remotely technically feasible, we can see similar patterns emerging on various on-line networks today. Sexual bulletin boards and the like closely mirror this same suburban psycho-social pattern. They are anonymous; they allow participants to "interact" without fear of "real" consequences; they encourage expression that would be difficult if not impossible in a real setting.

Some of the more extreme theorists of Virtual Reality imagine a point at which it will be possible to hook-up a human being's actual brain and neurological system to a computer-governed interactive system, resulting in the instantaneous creation of an externalized Virtual Reality from a person's fantasies, desires, or wishes. Perhaps such a scenario is only the most recent incarnation of a familiar human (or male?) dream of magical wish-fulfillment. But it nevertheless raises interesting questions about the idea of desire itself. Does the idea of desire itself embody the concepts of longing, of the delay of wish fulfillment? How can we imagine the structure of a psychology beyond desire in a situation in which every wish could be instantaneously realized?

4. Most of the preceding analysis has been based not on
actual Virtual Reality situations, but rather on speculative
assessments of what Virtual Reality can be or will be. At
present, existing Virtual Reality installations are limited to
the military, the experiments of a small number of artists
(such as the Softworlds group), and a few arcade machines.
It should be emphasized that, at this point, it is impossible
to assess whether sophisticated Virtual Reality will become a
major new medium or remain a point of speculation in the
public imagination. The possibility of the commercial
development of Virtual Reality depends on the mundane
question of whether corporations will make available the
huge outlays of capital necessary for the development and
production of sophisticated new hardware and software, and
whether this new genre of experience can be successfully and
cost-efficiently marketed. In general, it seems to me impossible to predict whether or not any new technology will
become successful. To choose two simple examples: 3-D
movies never caught on; by contrast, stereo sound has
become a completely accepted world-wide standard.
Whether or not the overwhelming drama inherent to Virtual
Reality will have the necessary appeal in a culture that has
recently rejected the scale of the movie screen for that of the
television monitor seems open to question. On the other
hand, perhaps Virtual Reality will become an important
form in amusement parks—where people have traditionally
gone to experience spectacles of altered realities.

Nevertheless, the use of Virtual Reality by artists does seem,
even at present, to serve some concrete, definable purpose,
ironically not dissimilar to the way it is used by the military.
Both artists and military planners employ Virtual Reality as
an experimental space, a space in which ideas can be tested
without real world constraints. Both groups are also able to
envision the use of Virtual Reality without regard for the
viability of its commercial potential.

For artists, Virtual Reality is emerging primarily as a sculptural medium. Over the last decade, the new sophisticated
computers have been used by artists and architects in a
variety of ways to visualize and construct increasingly complex spaces—some of which are in fact unique to the
computer's world and would be impossible to create without

computer-aided techniques. Adding Virtual Reality hardware makes it possible for the "viewer" to feel that he or she
is moving around in such constructed spaces in a way that
further enhances their spatial and sculptural quality. Further,
Virtual Reality has broken new ground by making possible
the construction of spaces that would be either physically
unfeasible or overly costly to build in reality. A project like
The Imperial Message extends the ideas of both installation
and earth art into a fantasy of space by constructing an
immense imaginary landscape.

It has always seemed to me that much of the significant
architecture of this century has been made for the movies—
movie architecture is free from the practical constraints of
program, budget, and durability. Without these limitations,
the imaginary architecture of *Blade Runner* or *Batman* far
surpasses the visions of even the most extreme built architecture of the last decade. It seems that for artists, Virtual
Reality has the capacity to take over this role at the point
that the movies leave off.

Peter Halley is an artist and writer living in New York City.

Suggestions for Further Reading

BOOKS

Aukstakalnis, S., and D. Blatner. *Silicon Mirage: The Art and Science of Virtual Reality.* Berkeley: Peachpit Press, 1992.

Benedikt, M., ed. *Cyberspace: First Steps.* Cambridge MA: MIT Press, 1991.

Benjamin, W. "The Work of Art in the Age of Mechcanical Reproduction." In *Illuminations,* trans. Harry Zohn, ed. Hannah Arendt. New York: Schocken Books, 1976.

Cironcione, J., and B. D'Amato, eds. *Through the Looking Glass: Artists' First Encounters with Virtual Reality.* Jupiter, Florida: Softworlds, 1992. Published in association with the exhibition at the Jack Tilton Gallery, New York.

Cotton, B., and R. Oliver. *Understanding Hypermedia: From Multimedia to Virtual Reality.* London: Phaidon Press, and San Francisco: Chronicle Books, 1993.

Crary, J., and S. Kwinter, eds. *Incorporations.* New York: Urzone, 1992.

DeLanda, M. *War in the Age of Intelligent Machines.* New York: Zone Books, 1991.

Feenberg, A. *Critical Theory of Technology.* New York: Oxford University Press, 1991.

Gibson, W. *Neuromancer.* New York: Berkley Publishing Group, 1984.

Hanhardt, J., ed. *Video Culture: A Critical Investigation.* Rochester: Visual Studies Workshop, 1986.

Heim, M. *The Metaphysics of Virtual Reality.* New York: Oxford University Press, 1993.

Ihde, D. *Technology and the Lifeworld: From Garden to Earth.* Bloomington: Indiana University Press, 1990.

Jacobson, L. *Garage Virtual Reality.* Indianapolis: Sams Publishing, 1994.

Jacobson, L., ed. *Cyberarts: Exploring Art and Technology.* San Francisco: Miller-Freeman, 1992.

Kruger, M. *Artificial Reality II.* Reading MA: Addison-Wesley Publishing Company, 1991.

Landow, G. P. *Hypertext: The Convergence of Contemporary Critical Theory and Technology.* Baltimore and London: The John Hopkins University Press, 1992.

Laurel, B. *Computers as Theatre.* Reading MA: Addison-Wesley Publishing Company, 1991.

Laurel, B., ed. *The Art of Human-Computer Interface Design.* Reading MA: Addison-Wesley Publishing Company, 1990.

Levidow, L., and K. Robins, eds. *Cyborg Worlds.* London: Free Association Books, 1989.

Lovejoy, M. *Postmodern Currents: Art and Artists in the Age of Electronic Media.* Ann Arbor MI and London: UMI Research Press, 1989.

Midgley, M. *Wisdom, Information and Wonder: What Is Knowledge For?* London: Routledge, 1989.

Noble, D. *Forces of Production.* New York: Alfred A. Knopf, 1984.

Penley, C., and A. Ross, ed. *Technoculture.* Minneapolis: University of Minnesota Press, 1991.

Rheingold, H. *The Virtual Community: Homesteading on the Electronic Frontier.* Reading MA: Addison-Wesley Publishing Company, 1993.

Rheingold, H. *Virtual Reality.* New York: Summit Books, 1991.

Weiner, N. *The Human Use of Human Beings.* 2d ed. Boston: Free Association Press, 1989.

Weizenbaum, J. *Computer Power and Human Reason.* San Francisco: W. H. Freeman, 1976.

Woolley, B. *Virtual Worlds: A Journey in Hype and Hyperreality.* Cambridge MA: Blackwell Publishers, 1992.

Zuboff, S. *In the Age of the Smart Machine: The Future of Work and Power.* New York: Basic Books, 1988.

PERIODICALS

Leonardo, published five-times per year (February, April, June, August, and October) by MIT Press.

Mondo 2000, published quarterly by Fun City Mega Media.

NewMedia, published monthly by Richard Landry/Hypermedia Communications, Inc.

Presence: Teleoperators and Virtual Environments, published quarterly by MIT Press.

Wired, published monthly by Wired Ventures Limited.

A Note on the Exhibition

Major support for the development of *Softworld 2.1: The Imperial Message* and for the presentation of this exhibition has come from the Wexner Center Residency Award program, funded by the Wexner Center Foundation, and from the Battelle Endowment for Technology and Human Affairs.

The development and presentation of *The Imperial Message* also have been made possible by the generosity of several corporate sponsors. The Kubota Pacific Corporation manufactures the high-end, real-time geometry and texture processor utilized in the creation of the project. The original model, animated sequences, and textures were produced by Blue Sky Productions' proprietary rendering system. The video projection cubes on which visitors see *The Imperial Message* have been provided by Sony Corporation. Real-time simulation software has been provided by Sense 8 Corporation. Elias Associates produced and designed the sound. The Head-Mounted Displays, or feed-back immersion helmets, have been provided by Virtual Research. IBM donated the PC used to process the sound. Imtech Corporation provided the video processor for the projection cubes; Polhemus, Inc., the position sensors for the Head-Mounted Displays; MicroSoft Corporation, a variety of software; Crystal River Engineering, the 3-D sound board; and Phar Lap Software, a DOS-extender for the PC.

During the exhibition at the Wexner Center, *The Imperial Message* was presented as a "work-in-progress": visitors had opportunities to comment on how the program works, and their comments will be utilized as Softworlds develops the final version of the project. *Softworld 1.2: Sacrifice* was available for play in a separate display.

Residency and Education Programs

Softworlds, Inc. is the recipient of the 1993–94 Wexner Center Residency Award in the visual arts. The residency awards program, supported by a continuing grant from the Wexner Center Foundation, was initiated to foster the arts of our time by encouraging and supporting the creative process. The awards are intended to provide artists with moral, financial, and technical support, as well as a suitable environment in which to create or complete new works. Every year, awards are given in each of the Wexner Center's program areas of performing arts, media arts, and visual arts. The artist or artists selected are then invited to work in residence at the Wexner Center, engaging students, faculty, and staff of The Ohio State University and the community at large.

Through the residency awards program, the Wexner Center seeks to encourage creative exchange on several levels. Artists in residence are able to draw upon the resources and expertise available at the university and in the community, while also learning about the interests and ideas of students, faculty, staff, and community members, who—in turn—are stimulated by the opportunity to work with the visitors. Specific residency projects and activities reflect the variety of award recipients' interests, disciplines, and working methods. Some artists meet with large groups of students and/or members of the community in workshops or classes. Others work closely with smaller numbers of students or volunteers, directly involving them in the realization of projects. Still others develop their projects in relative solitude, yet produce works of high visibility and broad appeal. By encompassing this range of approaches, the residency awards program is able to offer support to a full spectrum of creative endeavors and to expose the Wexner Center's audience to the diversity that is at the heart of contemporary art.

The members of Softworlds met with a number of university and community groups in the course of several visits to Ohio State during the 1993–94 academic year. Informal meetings with representatives of Ohio's Center of Science and Industry (COSI) and the university's Advanced Computing Center for the Arts and Design (ACCAD), Center for Cognitive Science, Center for Interdisciplinary Studies in Art and Design, College of the Arts, and Department of Computer and Information Science sparked wide-ranging discussions of artificial intelligence, "digital ethics," and experiences with various hardware and software. At two "Beta-Test" workshops, guests played *Sacrifice*, previewed parts of *The Imperial Message*, and provided the members of Softworlds with feedback on their reactions to each work. Brian D'Amato of Softworlds also participated as a speaker in the "Technology and Postmodern Culture" lecture series presented by the Center for Interdisciplinary Studies in Art and Design and cosponsored by the Wexner Center, the College of the Arts, and the Departments of Art, Industrial Design, Art Education, History of Art, and Architecture. The development of *The Imperial Message* was one of the topics touched upon in D'Amato's talk, "Interactivity, Freedom, and Mind Control."

Residency activities such as those described above offered the Wexner Center's audience direct and immediate insights into Softworlds' ideas and working methods. Other education programs, including a panel discussion on "Art and Culture in the Age of Interactive Technology," opened the discussion to a broader range of issues that placed Softworlds' projects in context. Panelists were Roy Ascott, Director of the Centre for Advanced Inquiry in the Interactive Arts (CAIIA) at the Newport School for Art and Design, Gwent College, Wales; Andrew Feenberg, Professor of Philosophy at San Diego State University; Constance Penley, Professor of Film Studies/Women's Studies at the University of California, Santa Barbara; and science-fiction author and journalist Bruce Sterling, who contributes frequently to *Wired*. The moderator was Allucquere Rosanne Stone, Assistant Professor of Radio, Television, and Film at the University of Texas, Austin. The panel discussion, which was held on May 13, was organized and coordinated by the Wexner Center's education department, which also presented tours for visitors of all ages throughout the duration of the exhibition.

During spring quarter 1994, a graduate-level course ("Interdisciplinary Research Seminar in Computer Technology in the Arts: Focus on Virtual Environments") offered through the College of the Arts at the Advanced Computing Center for the Arts and Design focused on virtual reality, interactivity, telecommunications, and associated topics. Taught by Carol Gigliotti, Assistant Professor of Art Education and Education and Technology Liaison for the Wexner Center, the seminar provided creative and technical support for participating students' individual projects or research. Developed in concert with the Softworlds residency, the course incorporated a discussion with the artists and examinations of their work but moved beyond that narrow focus, finding in Softworlds' projects springboards to related issues and concerns.

Education programs related to the Softworlds exhibition were made possible by the Ohio Joint Program in the Arts and Humanities and the Battelle Endowment for Technology and Human Affairs. The panel discussion was also generously supported by the university's Center for Interdisciplinary Studies in Art and Design. In addition, grant funding from the Battelle Endowment for Technology and Human Affairs supported a program in which gallery assistants, many of them university students, staffed the exhibition whenever it was open. The gallery assistants were available to help visitors operate the Head-Mounted Displays, video projection cubes, and touch-screen monitors used to play *The Imperial Message* and *Sacrifice*.

Artists' Biographies

Janine Cirincione was born in New York City in 1961. Her educational background is in French literature: she earned her BA degree in that field from City University of New York in 1984 and her MA degree from Hunter College in 1986. Since 1988 she has been the director of Jack Tilton Gallery in New York City, where she is now a partner. She previously worked as acquisitions and research editor at Art Resource and as director of archives and public information for the Pace Gallery, both also in New York. She has curated numerous exhibitions for Jack Tilton Gallery, among them *10 Latino Artists* (1988), *When Objects Dream and Talk in Their Sleep* (1991), *Forbidden Games* (1991), and *Through the Looking Glass: Artists' First Encounters with Virtual Reality* (1992). She was also the curator of *Dark Decor* (1991–93), an exhibition organized by Independent Curators, Inc. that travelled throughout the United States and Canada. She has contributed interviews and essays to *Cover Arts Magazine*, *Flash Art*, and *A Gathering of the Tribes*, where she serves on the Board of Directors. She has also lectured on art, technology, and new media at universities, museums, and conferences throughout the United States.

Brian D'Amato studied painting and English at Yale University, earning a BA in art. He subsequently studied painting and contemporary art history at the City University of New York, where he received his MA. In 1989 and 1990 he co-directed 65 Thompson Street Gallery for Leo Castelli and Larry Gagosian. He has exhibited his work in New York City and elsewhere (including in the Wexner Center's 1992 *Reframing Cartoons* exhibition) and contributed articles and reviews to *Flash Art*, *Harper's Bazaar*, and other publications. He participated in the 1992 exhibition *Through the Looking Glass* at the Jack Tilton Gallery and co-edited the accompanying catalogue with Janine Cirincione. D'Amato is also a novelist. *Beauty*, his first novel—an art-world thriller about cosmetic surgery—was published in the United States in October 1992 by Delacorte. *Beauty* has also been released in eight foreign editions, including a United Kingdom edition; the U.S. paperback edition was released in September 1993 by Dell, and a film version is in development at Touchstone Pictures. D'Amato is currently working on a second novel.

Michael Ferraro was born in 1953 in Passaic, New Jersey. During the 1970s he exhibited and performed interactive art pieces in galleries and museums. He earned his BFA in studio art from Syracuse University in 1976 and his MFA from the University of Massachusetts in 1980. He is currently on the faculty at the School of Visual Arts in New York, where he has taught in the area of computer art since 1989. He was previously a visiting artist and adjunct professor in the College of Fine Arts at Carnegie-Mellon University in Pittsburgh from 1983 to 1985. Since 1986 Ferraro also has been affiliated with Blue Sky Productions of Ossining, New York, as vice-president, system architect, and partner. He has been the technical director for numerous television commercials produced at Blue Sky Productions. He was also the technical director of computer animation for David Kronenberg's 1984 movie *The Fly* and the computer animation designer for a 1985 production of *The Odyssey* at Kresge Theater, Carnegie-Mellon University.

Softworlds, Inc. was founded in 1992. The group's works in progress include a CD-ROM publication, interactive role-playing games, and real-world sets.

Softworld 2.1: The Imperial Message

Created by Softworlds, Inc.:
Janine Cirincione, Brian D'Amato, and Michael Ferraro

Musical Score: Alvin Lucier
Images and Rendering: Blue Sky Productions
Sound: Elias Associates
Sound Design: Michael Sweet and Matt Fletcher
CGI Producer: Cindy Brolmsa
Modelling and Animation: Stewart Ziff; Cliff Bohm
     and Maurice Van Swaaij of Blue Sky Productions
User Interface Coordinator: Ethan Dicks
Programming Consultant: Matt Lewis

Voices
The Emperor: Steve Cannon
The Judges and Gulag Warden: Jim Chu
The Spy: Christian Haye
The Rebel: Cindy Brolmsa
The Messenger and Guide: Stephanie Jones
The Gatekeeper and Guide: Edwin Torres

Acknowledgments

We thank the following individuals for their support, assistance, and cooperation during the development of *Softworld 2.1: The Imperial Message* and in other aspects of our exhibition and residency at the Wexner Center: Roy Ascott, Bruce Bassett, Michael Benedikt, Cliff Bohm, Cindy Brolmsa, Stephanie Cadet, Steve Cannon, Wayne Carlson, Peter Carzasty, Bill Cook, Tom Coull, Ethan Dicks, Scott Elias, Andrew Feenberg, Matt Fletcher, Dave Franklin, Sherri Geldin, Carol Gigliotti, Timothy Greenfield-Sanders, Peter Halley, Kelly Halpine, Christian Haye, Barbara Helfer, Dave

Hinkle, Tom Jones, Jessica Josell, John R. Josephson, Mark Kettering, Larry Larson, Matt Lewis, David Lichtenstein, Alvin Lucier, Ellen Morris, Chuck O'Conner, Steve Organ, Constance Penley, Ken Pimentel, Tony Ramos, Luke Rawls, Dan Rice, Bill Rick, Sarah Rogers, Richard Roth, Susan Roth, Wes Shimanek, Todd Sines, Jack Smith, Bruce Sterling, Allucquere Rosanne Stone, Michael Sweet, Curtis Tearte, Maurice Van Swaaij, Barry Wine, Jaime Wolf, Evan Yeaman, Stewart Ziff, Eric Zimmerman, and all the people at the Wexner Center for the Arts and Ohio State. Special thanks to the partners at Blue Sky Projections—Alison Brown, David Brown, Carl Ludwig, Eugene Troubetzkoy, Chris Wedge—and to Jack Tilton and Susan Hort of the Jack Tilton Gallery.

In addition, we thank the many colleagues, friends, and family members who have been supportive of Softworlds and all our endeavors: Scott Baldinger, Robin Barnes, Francesco Bonami, Mary Boone, Evan Boorstyn, Peter Boris, Rob Boynton, Jacqueline Cantor, Brian Carl, Betsey Carter, Taro Chiezo, Amy Chosky, Marty & Lucy & Karl Cirincione, Judy Clain, Joanne Cohen, Joe Cohn, Anthony D'Amato, Barbara D'Amato, Paul D'Amato, Ellen Datlow, Andrew Druck, Bob & Val Ferraro, Gabe & Delores Ferraro, Richard & Angela Ferraro, Molly Friedrich, Dana Friis-Hansen, Carl Goodman, Michael Govan, Jonathan Gutenberg, Tom Hamrich, Marilee Heifitz, Peter Hort, Nick Jones, Helena Kontova, Molly Lafferty, Jackson Lewis, Allissa Loin, Christopher Makos, Laura Marks, Angela Matusik, Stephen Melville, James Meyer, Rick Montana, James S. Moore, Jacqueline Mori, Julie Oda, Celeste Olaquiaga, Robert Pincus-Witten, Dara Pizutti, David Polinchok, Tina Potter, Bernadine Rock, P. J. Rogers, Leslie Schnur, Kate Shanley, Junko Shimada, Michael Siegel, Pamela Singh, Andrew Solomon, Michael Spertus, Alisa Tager, Kevin Teixeira, Anna Wagner, Benjamin Weil, Morris Wheeler, and Alice Yang.

Janine Cirincione
Brian D'Amato
Michael Ferraro
Softworlds, Inc.

STAN MACK'S REAL LIFE FUNNIES

VIRTUAL KAFKA

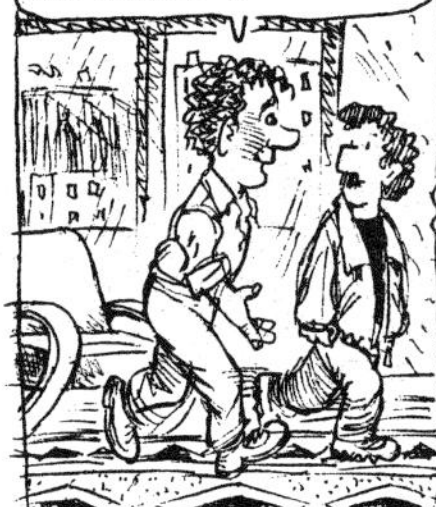

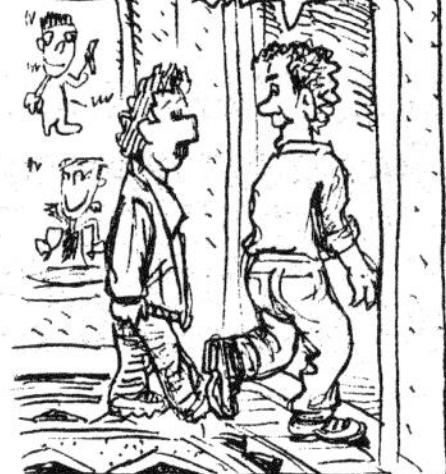

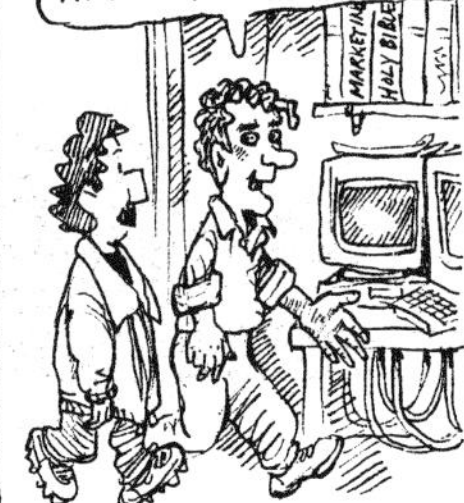

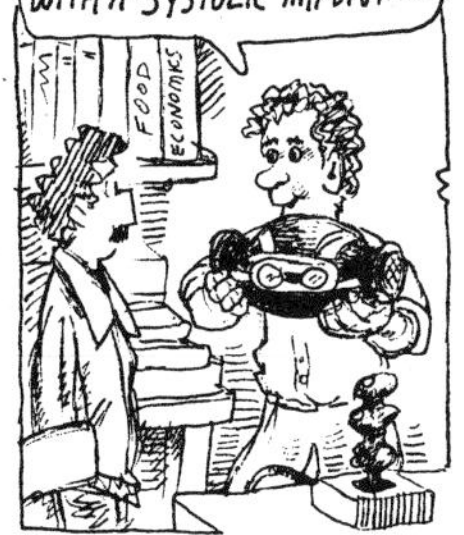

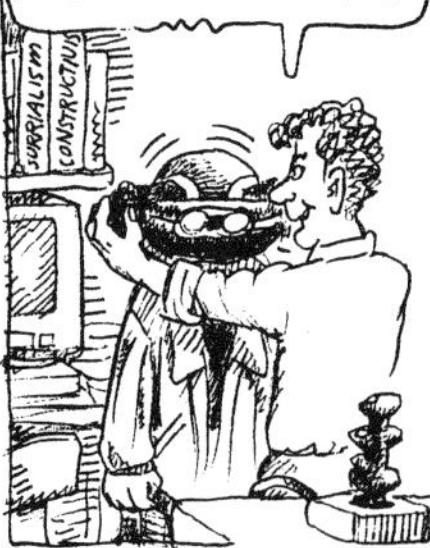

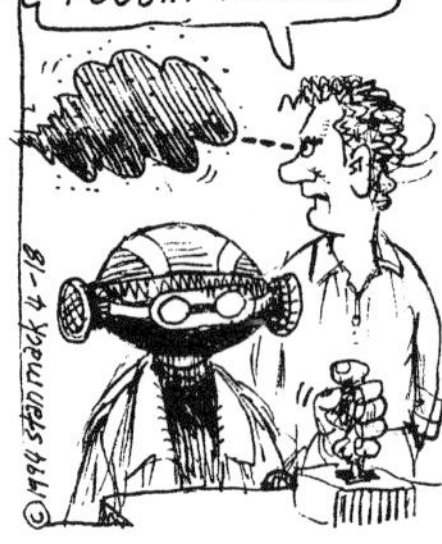

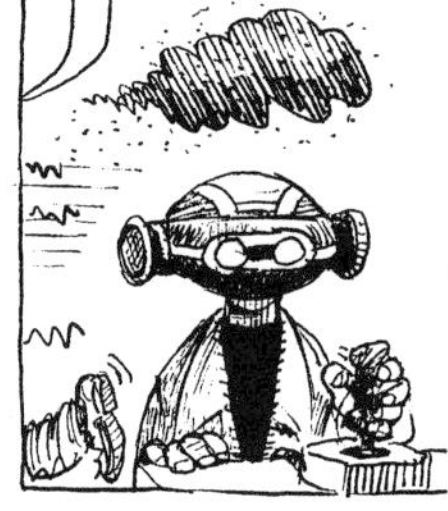

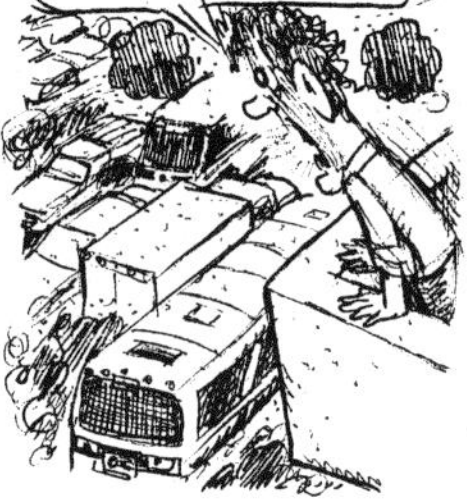

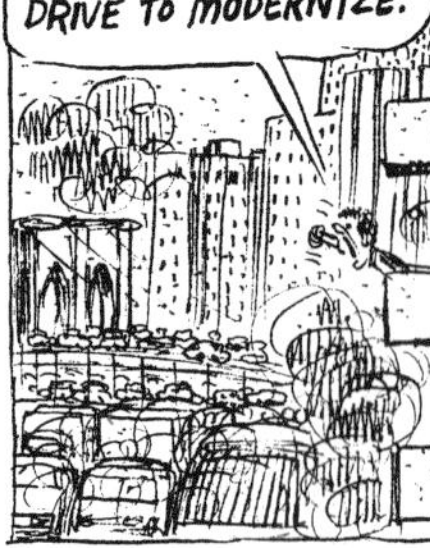

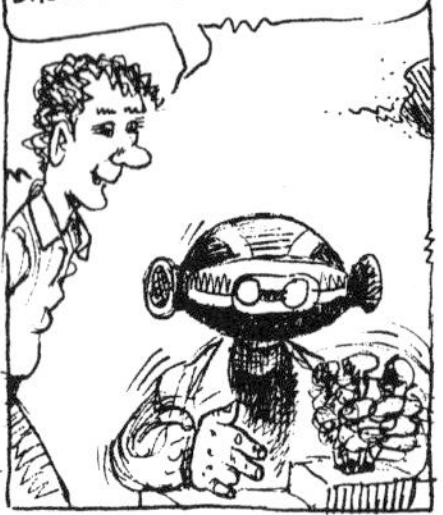